23 1/2 DEGREES AWAY FROM GOD

God Bless You Danielle

Fr. S...

Copyright © 2024 by James M. Sullivan
email: authorfr.jimsullivan@gmail.com

All rights reserved. No part of this publication may be reproduced, distributed, or transmitted in any form or by any means, including photocopying, recording, or other electronic or mechanical methods, without the prior written permission of the publisher, except in the case of brief quotations embodied in critical reviews and certain other noncommercial uses permitted by copyright law.

Scripture texts in this work are taken from the New American Bible, revised edition, © 2010, 1991, 1986, 1970 Confraternity of Christian Doctrine, Washington, D.C. All rights reserved.

Excerpts are taken from the English translation of the Catechism of the Catholic Church, Second Edition, © 1994, 1997, 2000 by Libreria Editrice Vaticana-United States Catholic Conference, Washington, D.C. All rights reserved.

The photographs on both the front and back covers are of the crosses at Holy Land Waterbury, USA at sunrise, contributed by John Sullivan.

All images in the book except for the one on page 158 are owned by the author.

Published by Highbury Press.
Layout and graphic design by Michael Griffin of Highbury Press.

IGHBURY PRESS

Printed in the United States of America
First Printing, 2024

ISBN: 979-8-9921707-0-2

Basilica of the Immaculate Conception
74. W. Main Street,
Waterbury CT 06702
www.waterburybasilica.org

23 1/2 DEGREES AWAY FROM GOD

Returning to the Light

Fr. Jim M. Sullivan

DEDICATION

To my loving parents, Jim and Phyllis Sullivan, in thanksgiving for planting the seeds of faith in my life, this book is lovingly dedicated. Their simplicity of life and trust in God has inspired me to live as they did.

And to the city that I love, Waterbury, Connecticut, the home of Blessed Michael McGivney, founder of the Knights of Columbus, and at one time the most Catholic city in the United States, I also dedicate this book. May our families and our cities always grow in love of God and neighbor.

ACKNOWLEDGEMENTS

I would like to acknowledge those who have been instrumental in the publication of this book. First and foremost, profound thanks go to parishioner, Dottie Daniels, for her tireless editorial assistance.

From editing, proofreading, typing, photos, computer skills, and overall moral support, gracious thanks are also expressed to Dan Mathews, GraceAnne Mitzel, Aurora Daly, Christa Chodkowski, Fr. John Gancarz (reviewer of manuscript), and Mike Griffin of Highbury Press.

CONTENTS

- Preface 11
- Chapter 1: *Less Is More*.. 15
- Chapter 2: *Faith and Father Cross the Ocean*...................... 27
- Chapter 3: *God Is Big on the Little* 35
- Chapter 4: *"Here I Am Lord:" Even in the Snow* 41
- Chapter 5: *Upon This Rock*... 45
- Chapter 6: *Five Ways To Conversion*..................................... 49
- Chapter 7: *Broken Butterfly*.. 61
- Chapter 8: *Always More Of That*... 69
- Chapter 9: *"Is This Not the Carpenter's Son?"*..................... 77
- Chapter 10: *Light and Heavy Burdened*............................... 85
- Chapter 11: *Tearing Down Is Easy; Let's Build* 93
- Chapter 12: *It Fits Like a Glove*.. 97
- Chapter 13: *Life to the Fullest, Cum Passio*......................... 111
- Chapter 14: *"Friend, Move Up Higher" (Luke 14:10)* 115
- Chapter 15: *Unless You Become Like a Child*.................... 119
- Chapter 16: *Strong and Gentle*... 129
- Chapter 17: *The Rain Is Gone*... 139
- Chapter 18: *Hurtful. Heavy. Holy.*....................................... 145
- Chapter 19: *Broken, Yet Whole* 151
- Chapter 20: *The Caution Of Conversion* 155
- Chapter 21: *Mend Your Nets*... 165

PREFACE

If the title of a book needs to be explained, perhaps it is not the greatest idea for a title. After all, titles of books, including creative ones, at least give a hint as to what the content of the book might be. You may be thinking, "How in the world do 23 1/2 degrees have anything to do with God?" Degrees generally refer to science, math, or temperature.

Back in my Providence College days, my uncle, Fr. John McMahon, O.P., a Dominican friar, teacher, and administrator, once gave a homily at Mass explaining why Christmas Day was celebrated on December 25th. Like most people, I assumed it was a well-known fact that Jesus was born on that day. Come to find out, at my then young age, it is not a fact at all. The Church does not know the exact date of Christ's birth.

It is possible that His birth did not occur in the winter, because it states in the Gospel of Luke that "Shepherds were in the field, watching their flock by night (Luke 2:8)." Some would argue that shepherds would not be spending as much time in the fields "watching their flocks by night" (Luke 2:8) in the colder northern hemisphere temperatures of December 25th. My uncle explained all of this in his homily, and then he continued to preach that the date of Christmas is based on the winter solstice.

You see, in pagan culture at the time of Christ, there was already a well-established great day of celebration on December 25th. Four days prior to that, December 21st (the winter solstice) is the day with the most darkness and the least amount of light. The pagan culture, seeing that each day prior to December 21st was becoming darker and darker, feared that if the darkness continued, it would result in the end of life itself. Without advanced science, the naked eye, after approximately four days, can determine that the days are actually getting longer. Light is coming back, darkness is reversed, and life will continue. The "gods" (they thought) were appeased, and as a result, the fourth day after the winter solstice each year, namely December 25th, became a day for great celebration.

Some scholars would have argued that when the early Christian missionaries began to preach and spread the Gospel of Jesus Christ, they found this deeply ingrained celebration of the sun (of light) already well-established in the minds and hearts of people. In their wisdom, the missionaries essentially Christianized a pagan holiday. They explained to the pagan people that Christ is the true Light of the World, the One who conquered the darkness, especially the darkness of sin and death. Instead of worshiping the sun in the sky, the missionaries taught them to worship the true Light of the World, the Son of God, Jesus Christ. As the expression goes, "the rest is history." And so, December 25th, from antiquity, became the great day of celebration for the birth of Christ.

Science tells us that the earth tilts 23 1/2 degrees on its axis away from the sun. On December 21st, (again, the day with the most darkness and the least amount of light), the earth begins to realize greater and greater light. We all know, from our own experience of weak and fallen human nature, that the human person also "tilts" away from the Light — that Light, of course, being God. Even a child, generally at around the age of seven or eight years old (known as the age of reason), begins to distinguish the difference between right and wrong.

From that time on, as a result of our fallen human nature and original sin, the tilt from God escapes no one. We are all sinners, yet the degree of the tilt varies from person to person. For those very saintly people, the degree of the tilt may be small; for others, a greater degree, and for still others, "23 1/2 degrees" or perhaps beyond. The earth, for countless millennia, has consistently tilted only so far. The human person, on the other hand, because of one's sinful nature, is able to fall (tilt) far away from God —far beyond 23 1/2 degrees— sometimes to a point of being spiritually "flat-lined."

Sadly, we then find ourselves essentially becoming dead in our spirits. The point of return, essentially a turning away from sin and self-deception, unlike the annual precision of the earth, comes at different times in a person's life. For some, the realization of the existence of a loving God is already implanted in the heart from their earliest years. For others, it comes in college or young adulthood. For still others, Christ becomes "real" after the birth of a child or an experience of great beauty. Some people return to a life of faith after tragedy, others in the autumn or winter years of life, and sadly, the return for others never really comes. Yet, the Light of Christ and the breath of God is continually present and never ceases to call humanity back to that place of light and peace.

The following pages are partly my own story and my surprise calling to the priesthood in the fifth decade of my life. Beyond my own life experience in the working world (for some thirty years) and now through ten years of priesthood, I've primarily written about the call to conversion: the call that hopefully all of us have had or will soon experience — a call to God who is the source of love and life itself. The working world in the contracting profession, prior to my call to the priesthood, has helped immensely in my understanding of both the weaknesses and strengths of human nature. Above all that, the powerful love of God and His transforming grace enables all of us to move from wherever we are in our spiritual lives to return to the Light and discover the true meaning and purpose of life.

The Basilica of the Immaculate Conception, where I am currently rector, has a parish history dating back to 1847. We are among the first established churches in the State of Connecticut and the home parish of Blessed Michael McGivney, founder of the Knights of Columbus. Blessed Michael McGivney was a model priest who loved his vocation, loved to serve the people of God, and had a special love for the family.

In decades past, Waterbury, Connecticut has also been described as the most Catholic city in the United States (per capita). With a population of just over 100,000, there were twenty Catholic churches, ten grade schools, four Catholic high schools, and a large Catholic hospital. Growing up here as a child, I thought there was only one faith! I pray that all those reading these pages, whether Catholic, non-Catholic, or of little or no belief, will in some way experience the "tilt" of their lives changed to one of greater closeness to the true Light of the World: Jesus Christ.

LESS IS MORE — 1

It was rather simple. Primitive, actually. This was life on a little island in southwest Ireland, called Fenit Island. Fenit Island is eight miles south of the well-known city of Tralee. Fenit is where my father grew up. Primitive, indeed: no running water, no electricity or refrigeration, no plumbing of any kind, an outhouse, a pot over a large fireplace for cooking, tiny rooms, and a dirt floor. The exterior was simple too: stucco walls and the traditional thatched roof, typical of so many of Ireland's homes at that time.

Life on the island was difficult, but difficult is a relative term. In order to simply survive, humanity adapts and does what needs to be done. The O'Sullivans (my family name in Ireland) operated an eighty-acre farm: potatoes (of course), sugarcane, barley, pigs, and some head of cattle. Ireland's regular rain and misty weather was standard fare. The mid-1800's house was built near an imposing fifteen-foot rock cliff overlooking the ocean. My father would often say with his sweet Irish brogue, "The Atlantic was lappin' at me back door!"

The family worked hard, and farming, especially before modern tractors, was so much more difficult. My father and his three brothers tilled the soil each year, led by a team of horses. Dad would often say, "I was pickin' potatoes before I was walkin'!" Though Dad would often put a little Irish tale at the end of his stories, there may have actually been some truth to that statement. The entire family worked the farm—they had to. Like so many farming families, their livelihood depended on it.

While so many Irish emigrated during the tragic Potato Famine of the 1840s to 1850s, the O'Sullivans never did. My father was the first in his family to move to the United States. The Potato Famine devastated so many families, yet because of the proximity of the farm to the ocean, our family always had food. If fish was needed for supper, my father would simply go to the back of the house, drop a line off the rocks, and within seconds, a good-sized pollock or haddock was caught fresh for the family meal. Rabbits were also plentiful, and rabbit traps regularly provided dinner. Cows provided plenty of milk, and there were chickens and pigs, too.

The soil on the island was seemingly different from anywhere else in Ireland. As waves crashed on the rock cliffs surrounding Fenit Island, a fine, salty mist acting as a sort of fertilizer covered the land; the Potato Famine did not affect the crop the same way it did in other parts of Ireland. It has been said that potatoes from Fenit Island are among the finest in all of Ireland. Therefore, while at the time of the famine, many in Ireland were starving, the O'Sullivans were not, and I'm sure that is the reason they stayed on the island and did not need to abandon their home to find livelihood elsewhere.

These few paragraphs set the stage for what life was like, at least in this remote part of Ireland, during the late 1920s, '30s, and '40s. To all of us now living in the 21st century, this primitive lifestyle may appear to be what life was like in the 1400s. The way so many people in the world lived just eighty years ago is unimaginable to society's modern mind.

Fenit Island has also been described as one of the most beautiful places in Ireland. The 400-acre parcel (of which the O'Sullivan's farmed approximately eighty acres) was nestled at the base of a stunningly beautiful mountain range called Slieve Mish. The mighty waves of the Atlantic pounded on the western side, while at the same time on the opposite side of the property, the island possessed a serene, quiet inlet that gave the feeling of being hugged — yes, even by a landscape. The ruins of a ninety-foot tall, fourteenth-century castle with two sides destroyed centuries ago by Oliver Cromwell proudly stands over the bay. Amidst the difficulty of life and work, the island was also a beautiful and peaceful refuge, a place where one could pray and meditate and find peace in daily life.

Fenit Castle ruins

What made life on the island not only bearable, but even joyful, was the faith that the families shared. The majority of Ireland at that time was living the Catholic faith. Often called "the Land of Saints and Scholars," Ireland provided missionaries to every corner of the world. Two of them were my own aunts, Sr. Mary Melbride and Sr. Mary Cataldas, who left the island together at the ages of seventeen and fifteen to be missionaries in Australia in the 1930's. Not knowing if the family would ever see them again, prior to departing, they cut some of their hair and placed it in a vase. For decades, that vase remained on the mantle of that simple home as a reminder of their love and devotion.

My aunts, Sr. Mary Melbride and Sr. Mary Cataldas (circa 1940s)

The great Irish missionary, Fr. Patrick Peyton, coined the phrase so well known, but seldom practiced: "The family that prays together, stays together." Life at that time—on the farm, and in the cities—was a life of faith in Jesus. Faith was in the air, in the very life and breath of society. Everything centered on the parish. It was an unusual person who did not practice a life of faith. My father vividly recalls walking the eight miles from Tralee to Fenit on a cool summer evening, and while doing so, hearing through the open windows from house after house, the Rosary being prayed. How times and events have changed in such a short period of history!

The parish which all the locals attended was the Church of the Purification, a church seating 250, nestled in a serene and quiet country setting and overlooking Fenit Bay. The faithful would make great efforts to attend Sunday Mass. Horse and buggy was the standard mode of transportation, with rain and wet weather often being the norm.

My father's childhood parish: Church of the Purification

Thus far, I have been referring to the land where the O'Sullivans lived as Fenit Island. That, indeed, is the name. These 400 acres were home to approximately fifteen to twenty families, all of them farmers. Although named an "island," there is a small strip of land that connects the island to the mainland. At low tide, horse and carriage were able to bring milk and other products to market. The family would often have to rise early in the morning to milk the cows, so as not to be prevented from traveling by the incoming tide.

Church on Sunday was important: in fact, more important than any other activity. Although my grandfather died when my dad was still a teenager, his mom saw to it that the faith was lived. Along with so many other families in Ireland, the O'Sullivans prayed the Rosary nightly. On their knees on the dirt floor, bead after bead glided through their fingers. To my knowledge, the question, "Do we have to?" was never asked. Prayer was simply a part of life, as is eating, drinking, sleeping, and working. Faith was not practiced "when I have the time." The worship of God was as regular as the rising sun, the shifting of tides, and the waves crashing on the coast.

My father told a humorous childhood story. He and his brothers opened up a small section of fence separating the adjacent farm. The neighbor, Mr. Murphy, could be seen by my grandmother charging across the fields with his red-faced indignation because his cattle were now passing through the fallen gate. Anticipating the likelihood of a difficult encounter, my grandmother quickly gathered the family to their knees and began praying the Rosary.

Mr. Murphy came to the door, entered without knocking, and saw the entire family praying. With great hesitation, but also out of respect, he, too, knelt down, took off his cap, and began to pray the Rosary with the family. Looking at him from the corner of her eye, seeing him still upset and red-faced, she began (after the Rosary), to pray the Litany of the Saints. The prayers continued until a calm demeanor emerged.

After the prayers, she spoke up in her beautiful Irish accent, "Now, Mr. Murphy, what is it that I can do for you?" Now calm due to the prayer, he replied, "Nah, Mrs. O'Sullivan, it's okay. Maybe if you could just tell the boys to be a little more careful with the fence." "Mr. Murphy, I'll sure see to it that they do," was her reply. How prayer brings peace to the soul!

Aerial view of Fenit Island

Sunday morning was, of course, a special day, the Lord's Day, and traveling to Mass was not easy. The entire family (a total of nine) would get into the horse-drawn carriage and ride along the beach, often atop compacted seaweed. The thin strip of sand connecting the mainland was followed by an additional two miles, and then the final incline to the parish. When high tide prevented land travel, the entire family would instead get into a large rowboat, made by my grandfather, and would row three-quarters of a mile across the bay, then walk the remaining distance up the hill to the church. As a young boy, I remember being very impressed by this story: the resolve, the dedication, and ultimately the love of my grandparents in seeing that the family attended Holy Mass — together.

Like many Irish who are wonderful storytellers, my dad, too, was known to embellish his stories from time to time. In the Irish persona, embellishing is not at all lying, nor is it making something up. Embellishing adds a bit of interest to a story, gives the story some flair, and piques one's attention, especially if the story is well told. And so, whenever my siblings or I heard stories of "heroism," a little part of that interior voice asked, "Really, Dad? I wonder if that's exactly the way it happened."

**My dad, James, with his seaside bounty,
Fenit Island (1944)**

Any of my own doubts about his exaggerated stories quickly came to an end when in 2016 as a newly ordained priest, I went to visit my father's farm and homestead. I wanted to see, firsthand, the roots from where my own faith began. Near the farm is Fenit Pier. It is a small commercial shipping area on the mainland. Later that same day, a ninety-six-year-old man saw me dressed in my priestly clerics while standing on the pier, facing the beautiful water and Slieve Mish Mountains. He must have heard that the son of Jamie O'Sullivan became a priest and was visiting. He approached me and immediately shared that he knew my father. My father had left the island for the United States some sixty years earlier. He continued, saying twice, "I knew your father. I knew your father. On Sunday mornings, your family would get into the boat, row across the bay, dock at my aunt and uncle's yard, and walk up the hill to the church." I could not help but immediately think, "Wow, my father really was telling the truth!" No *tale* in that story.

As beautiful as the faith of mothers and grandmothers is, and as integral as their love of God is to the formation of faith in their children and grandchildren, statistics show that it is the faith life of the father that most inspires. Children want to see their father as a hero—as the best dad in the world. On one occasion, when I was a little boy, a group of us was playing outside and we were all yelling to each other, "My dad is better than your dad!" Intuitively, we want to see our fathers as people who live beyond themselves—for something, ultimately for Someone—greater. The person who lives primarily for himself is indicating, simply by the way he lives, what is most important in life, and that this world and the things of this world hold the greatest importance. It is fair to say that men, overall, have dropped the ball, and tend to be very weak when it comes to spiritual matters.

We all know that in today's modern world, there is a crisis of fatherhood. Absentee fathers, the sadness of broken families, and fatherless homes are all too often the norm. In our weak and fallen world, a man can often find himself living as much for himself as for his family and children. Selfishness is poison to a family and distorts the very reason and purpose of why we are on earth. The antidote to living a life more for self than for others is to live a life of self-sacrifice.

St. Paul, in his letter to the Philippians, calls it "an emptying of self" — in Greek, a *kenosis*. When we are filled with self, we are incapable of also living fully for others. More of "me" means less of "you." More of me means less of God, too. Children of all ages ultimately desire a father who strives to be empty of self, a man who lives for a greater good and purpose. Our society, our Church, our world, has suffered from a disordered fatherhood. This needs to change, and when it does, all of society will rise to new and greater heights of love and devotion. President John F. Kennedy once said, "A rising tide lifts all boats." In the same way, rising fatherhood lifts the family. As Pope Saint John Paul II beautifully said, "As the family goes, so goes society, and so goes the whole world in which we live."

Nothing replaces the heart of a mother — *nothing*. Mothers are the ones who rarely give up on their children. Women also generally pray more than men, are more faithful than men, love God more than men, and attend church more than men. Not only mothers, but sisters can also have a great effect on the faith life of another (at least that has been the case for me).

I have a sister, Eileen, who was also very devout from her earliest years. After serving in the Air Force for seven years and specializing in both labor and delivery and cardiac rehab, she felt the call at age 38 to become a religious sister. She joined a relatively new community at that time called the Sisters of Life, and she took the name, Sr. Veronica. This community was initiated by Cardinal O'Connor in 1991 with the sole purpose of promoting the dignity of all human life, from conception to natural death.

With my sister, Eileen
(Sr. Veronica Mary of the Sisters of Life),
(2016)

Devout parents pray for their children, but so do devout siblings. I know that my sister prayed not only for me, but for my other brothers and sister as well, and I know that her prayers had a great effect on my life, and perhaps even helped me to recognize more clearly God's call to priesthood.

Back to the farm. Seeing the land, the farm, the house, the parish, the island, the old thatched cottage, was a throwback in time. Not only did my father not exaggerate, life on the island was actually much simpler and more primitive than I could have ever imagined. Over the course of sixty years of wind, and rain, and isolation, most of the roof deteriorated and caved in. I eagerly crossed the threshold of my grandparents' bedroom: the room where my father was born. Streams of sunlight peeked in through the broken rafters. An overpowering spirit of thanksgiving filled me. I got down on my knees, kissed the ground, and after finding a small, partially deteriorated table, celebrated Mass in the very room where my father was born.

Celebrating Mass in my father's house. (2015)

In a place reminiscent of the simplicity of the Christ-child's manger, Mass was celebrated. That room on that day was among the most beautiful "churches" in which I have ever had the privilege of celebrating Mass.

FAITH AND FATHER CROSS THE OCEAN 2

The farm, although large by some standards, was simply too small to support another family. My dad felt called to marriage and to raise a family of his own. As beautiful as the island was — land, cattle, scenic bay, mountain range, ocean, and sunset (Fenit Island's landscape belongs on a postcard or travel guide), raising an additional family in this environment would not have been financially possible. My father was the youngest of seven. His two older brothers and older sister never married, and they lived their entire lives on the farm. My father, being the youngest, may have felt like he was "under their thumb." The rainy weather was also tiresome, as was farming itself. So at the age of thirty-three, often called "the age of glory and of resurrection," and the fullness of manhood (the age of Christ's death and resurrection), my father traveled to Waterbury, Connecticut, where his aunt lived. And so he began a new life.

Life in the industrial city of Waterbury was vastly different from the country setting of the remote island. Dad experienced many firsts. He humorously recalled, with a little embarrassment, his first time entering a movie theater. As if he were entering a church, he instinctively genuflected before going into his seat! When he saw his first bowl of spaghetti, he nearly threw up, thinking it was a bowl of worms.

Work in Waterbury, Connecticut, was plentiful in the 1950s. The factories in the "Brass and Copper Capital of the World" were bustling with activity. If a person desired a job, he or she simply came to Waterbury, Connecticut and found a job, perhaps even the next day. Shortly after arriving, my dad sought employment at Platt Brothers,

Inc., one of the oldest manufacturers in Waterbury. You would never see this today, but even while applying for a factory job, my dad wore a suit and tie for the interview. The president of the company hired my father on the spot and asked, "When can you start?" My father, with excitement, said, "Right now!" The employer, delighted with his enthusiasm, told him to go home, change out of his suit, and, "Begin tomorrow morning." My dad was a great employee for thirty-three years until his retirement in 1986.

My mom was born in Waterbury's south end on Southview Street. Her parents were very devout people. Unlike my father's family, they never prayed together as a family; rather, each prayed quietly and more privately. This is the preferred way of prayer for so many. Even deeply spiritual people can experience a level of discomfort when praying out loud in the presence of others. They prefer private prayer, quiet time alone with God. Mass time is different. We're all together at Mass, and with a certain "flock mentality," we can feel more comfortable praying out loud.

One way of prayer is not necessarily better than the other, but admittedly, it is beautiful to witness people express their faith in a setting outside of church. Talking about God can become as natural and normal as talking about the news, or sports, or any other love of life.

We all need time alone too, time to be silent and with God. In a world occupied with so much noise and distraction, finding time to be quiet in the presence of God is essential. Although in different ways, prayer permeated the houses of my mom and dad. As young children, they already knew Jesus. How true it is that "the family that prays together stays together." Family prayer always bears fruit.

Waterbury is also home to Blessed Michael McGivney, the founder of the Knights of Columbus and if canonized, he will be the first U.S.-born diocesan priest to be canonized a saint. What an honor for his hometown, Waterbury, and his parish, Immaculate Conception!

I sometimes "pinch myself" thinking of the privilege of being the rector of the home parish of a potential saint. Born in 1852, Fr. McGivney's father, like my own father, also emigrated from Ireland to the U.S. seeking a better life. Patrick (his father) was a skilled metal worker. Both he and his wife Mary (Lynch) brought with them their deep Catholic faith.

Fr. McGivney's parents had a profound influence on his faith life. He grew up in Waterbury where the faith at that time was the very fabric of society, the very air he breathed. Already at his young age, he began to witness family hardship when the breadwinner of the household was unable to work due to illness or injury. Young, untimely deaths were also common at the time. Fr. McGivney's concern for the widow and orphan began from what he was already witnessing as a young boy.

Without the seeds of faith being sown through his parents, Michael's direction in life would have been very different. Not only "the family that prays together, stays together," but so often when the family prays together, children flourish and like Fr. McGivney, they can have a profound effect on the world.

May I urge everyone reading this book, if you are not already doing so, to pray together as a family. This can perhaps begin with something as simple as praying grace before meals and may later develop into praying the family rosary.

I was also born very close to the place where Fr, McGivney was born, and my entire family has a devotion to him. My uncle, Fr. John McMahon, a Dominican Friar at Providence College, essentially resurrected a defunct Knights of Columbus college council from a handful of men to over 550 members. For many years, my mother planted flowers at the McGivney family plot where his parents and several of his siblings are buried. I continue my mom's legacy and have also planted flowers at the graves of a number of priests for nearly three decades. Before she died, my mother had a vision of Fr. McGivney while she was praying in St. Thomas Church in Thomaston, Conn., the town where he died. I believe that this was a favor granted to my mother through his intercession and was his way of saying, "Thank you for taking care of my parents."

I, too, thank my mother and father for showering me with continual seeds of faith. Perhaps the many priests whose graves I adorned for many years, granted in return their own prayers for me. I believe that their prayers were instrumental in guiding me to my true calling, to follow them in the priesthood of Jesus.

With my mom, Phyllis, McGivney Family gravesite, Waterbury, Conn. (2016)

My parents met in 1955. My mom, Phyllis McMahon, had recently graduated from Belleview Hospital School of Nursing in New York City and was working at Waterbury Hospital. One day my dad, who was still pretty fresh "off the boat" from Ireland, came to the hospital to visit a man by the name of Jimmy Houlihan, a friend of his from the Irish-American Club. Jimmy was suffering from an ulcer. My mom was his nurse and while both were in the room, Jimmy said, "Neither of you are leaving this room until you make a date." They both initially refused, but finally gave in to his persistent request. Long story short, they had a wonderful marriage. My father would often say with a smile, "Thank God for Jimmy Houlihan's ulcer!"

When a young couple dates (in previous times, known as "courting"), they enjoy time together: walks, dinners, the beach, movies, shared hobbies, etc. My parents, like so many couples, enjoyed these things too. However, they had a very unusual Tuesday night date. At that time (late 1950s), a New York priest, scholar, and preacher named Bishop Fulton Sheen hosted a prime-time show entitled "Life Is Worth Living." The show was educational, inspirational, and even added humor in areas of faith, moral living, and current events. Over twenty million people tuned into this program every Tuesday evening. For my parents, it was their Tuesday night date.

When a couple shares a deep faith life, their chances for a successful and happy marriage are significantly higher. The reason, of course, is that the deepest and most important beliefs of life are held in common. It's wonderful when a couple enjoys similar hobbies and interests, likes, and dislikes; however, earthly interests only go so deep. After a period of time, they can even become old and stale. Golf is a great game, but golf does not satisfy the deepest drives of the heart. Dinner dates are very enjoyable, but they never satisfy the greatest hunger of all. In his Confessions, St. Augustine once said: "You have made us for yourself, Oh Lord, and our hearts are restless until they rest in You." Marriages of two different faiths can very often work out beautifully; however, nearly every priest or spiritual counselor would say that as one of the spouses grows more intimately in a relationship to Christ, he or she finds him/herself praying and hoping that the other spouse will find God too. Nothing in this world can substitute for the joy that can be found in Christ. If God is the source of all love, and marriage is a covenant of love, then the more a couple is connected to the source of love, the greater their married love will be.

We celebrate many weddings at the Basilica of the Immaculate Conception with over fifty couples always preparing at any given time. Marriage is one of my favorite ministries as a priest. From our very first meeting, I always remind the couple, while pointing to a crucifix on the wall, that Venerable Fulton Sheen once penned, "It takes three to marry." Many people in our society believe it takes only two to marry—the bride and the groom. Sadly, and all too often, marriages are more about the venue or the party. However, it is the Church, the blessing, and the Sacrament that is the most meaningful part of this special day.

I commend every couple for choosing to marry in a church, because, at some level, no matter where people are in their spiritual lives, whether they be closer to God or just starting off, they desire that ever-important third person, Christ Himself, to be in their marriage. The current world and culture distract people from living a life of faith, while instead encouraging a life in pursuit of "stuff" and of self. When this happens, love only grows so far. Marriages are best when Christ is invited to the feast.

Marriage is a covenant, and not simply a contract. We all know well what a contract is. Anyone in the working world makes agreements, business to business. We all have credit cards and sign contracts on the dotted line. We are not nearly as familiar with the word "covenant." From the first book of the Bible, Genesis, to the last book of the Bible, Revelation, we see the meaning of this word as a sacred bond. A contract denotes "This is mine, this is yours. I will do this, you will do that." A covenant speaks an entirely different language. It does not tout that "this is mine, this is yours," but rather that "I am yours, and you are mine."

A contract is an exchange of things. A covenant is an exchange of persons. A contract is 50/50. A covenant is 100/100 (I'm all in!). A contract is signed. A covenant is lived, shared, experienced. A contract and a covenant are miles apart from each other. In our secular world, many couples have been misled into believing that earthly love is all there is, and completely miss the greatest love of all — the love of God. If God is not the center of a marriage, something else will be. With Christ in the center of a marriage, the joys of life are multiplied, and the sorrows of life are diminished.

At every wedding, during the homily, I give a crucifix to the couple. With usually well over 100 people in attendance, I encourage all couples to place a crucifix in their home, preferably in their bedroom, and more specifically, above their bed. Christ will be that rock foundation and sacred "glue" that keeps a couple in love through both the joys and the sorrows of life. The marriage that my parents experienced was not a contract; it was a covenant — and Christ was at the center.

GOD IS BIG ON THE LITTLE

3

Most people who lived in the 1950s and earlier would agree that life was simpler then. My mother used to say, "We were all poor, but we didn't realize it." Nearly everyone in the greater Waterbury area worked in the factories, did their best to raise a family, and did their best to live a life of faith. Although by today's standards, most families were lower middle class, they took pride in their homes and apartments. My mom would say that even the streets were kept clean. Monsignor John Bevins, pastor of the Basilica for nearly twenty-four years, was born in the same year as my mom. He recalls, as she did, the iceman coming by horse-drawn carriage, and the children running after, picking up the ice chips to suck on. It is not as primitive as Fenit Island, but simple enough. My mom would often use the word innocence to describe the time she grew up in Waterbury.

Waterbury's icon, Msgr. John Bevins, beside a statue of World War II Navy chaplain, Fr. Thomas Conway (son of the Basilica) and recipient of the Navy Cross

My parents began their marriage in a very small, one-bedroom apartment on Cooke Street in Waterbury. I am the second child of six, and the reason my parents had to find a larger place. From 1960 (the year I was born) to 1967, my father's take-home pay was $70.02 per week. This was a standard factory worker's pay, but it was extremely difficult to raise a family of six children with that modest amount of money. My mother once prayed, "Lord, if you are going to give me all these children, you better give me a way to take care of them." Somehow, my parents, like many others at that time, were able to rub two nickels together and make a quarter. Many of our clothes came from $1 bag sales at Goodwill and church bazaars. My mom was a bit embarrassed by this and wished that if there was one thing she could change, it would be to have given us newer clothes. As children, we really didn't know the difference, and when the bags arrived, we would all enthusiastically fish through them. I still remember my favorite Goodwill yellow pullover sweater!

**St. Hedwig Grade School Baseball Team,
Naugatuck, Conn. (1970)**

During college summers, I worked at the same factory as my father, Platt Brothers. My work was primarily in the casting shop, loading furnaces with zinc. One day, a splash of molten zinc just missed my eye and landed on my hand where there is still a scar. I could have been permanently injured or blinded at eighteen years old, and I think of this from time to time. That would have changed my life so much. On another day, a 350-pound box fell on my foot, and believe it or not, I'm starting to feel the effects of it now at sixty-four years old.

Childhood injuries to the body, neck, back, knees—from sports, or otherwise—can sometimes come back to haunt us years later. Spiritual scars from the past can haunt us too. People often share with a priest their childhood sins or scars that either they brought upon themselves through mistakes and bad choices or the scars that others have caused. Unresolved scars —hurts that are kept inside— often show their painful face years later. If we don't give our wounds to Christ, in one way or another, they are given to another, often in the form of pain. As Pope Francis so often says, "God's name is Mercy." That mercy can heal even the deepest wounds. "God always forgives, people sometimes forgive, but nature never forgives."

During these summers, what impressed me so much about my father was his simple gratitude for having a job and raising a family. He would often come home from work whistling. As a young boy, I thought to myself, "Work must be fun!" My father called the factory that supported six children and two parents, "jolly 'ol Platt Brothers." He was definitely a company man. Making the little money that he did during those younger years, my father still believed that he was a rich man. It wasn't until later years that I realized what he meant and how truly rich he was.

Each day at Platt Brothers, when the coffee truck pulled up during morning break, many (if not most) of the men would patronize it.

Not once did my father go to the food truck, or for that matter, any of the vending machines. By spending money on himself, it meant less for the family. Beyond saving this little bit of money, it was for me a tremendous lesson in self-discipline, and in reality, self-donation.

It is not only important, but necessary in the spiritual life, to be able to say "no" to oneself. A person who is unable to say "no" to self will often find himself saying "yes" to the things he shouldn't, and "no" to the things he should affirm. Self-discipline leads to self-emptying, and when we are empty of self, we are then able to live beyond ourselves, to live for God and others. The four poisonous words of the spiritual life are I, me, my, and mine. If it's all about "me," it's not about "you," and it is certainly not about God either. We cannot, at the same time, be both filled with self and filled with God. One or the other diminishes. Philippians 2:6 says, "Christ emptied Himself, taking the form of a slave."

The world does not believe in saying "no" to self, nor does it see the advantage of "no" for a greater good. Saying "no" means depriving oneself of some pleasure (usually an immediate one) that we desire. Saying "no" can be painful. The earthly pleasures we seek, however, are generally very temporary, never lasting or completely satisfying. Saying "no" to self may be painful for the moment, but when it is done for a greater good and purpose, and especially as a prayer, it always brings inner peace.

We have all heard the expressions, "Youth is wasted on the young," and "If I only knew then what I know now." A humorous bumper sticker once read, "Hire a teenager while they still know everything." So often as children, we don't understand or appreciate the incredible self-sacrifice of parents: getting up in the morning, in the middle of the night, at times going to work exhausted, having to tend to the needs of a child at any and every hour. During these times, parents would give anything to simply have an hour for themselves, a simple moment of peace. Scott Hahn, the great Catholic evangelist, once said, "I did not realize how selfish I was until I got married and had children." His wife, Kimberly, is known to have said, "I strive for holiness one diaper at a time." Parenting can be a powerful means of achieving great sanctity.

From my earliest years, I remember God and Church being central to my parents' lives and therefore to the family. Some people live a "holier than thou, faith-on-the-sleeve" piety. This type of spirituality attracts very few people. What makes faith attractive is when it is lived authentically by normal, everyday working people who are filled with joy. We all desire happiness and when we see it lived and expressed in another person, we begin to say to ourselves, "I want what she has" or "What is it that makes him so happy?" When faith is seen as joyful, it is attractive.

Faith that is forced on another never takes root. It has to become one's own, a personal relationship with Christ. In other words, it has to be real—it has to be authentic. Our young people today are seeking authenticity, and they can sense artificiality from a mile away. When they see faith as real and meaningful and authentically joyful, they will begin to devote their entire lives to it. They (in fact all of us) have seen enough of the façade of happiness. They recognize that there is more to life than the glitter of technology and all the "stuff" of the world.

We are all fighting a worldly tsunami, a powerful tide that is sweeping many away from Christ. The world offers mediocrity at best, whereas Christianity offers authentic, true joy. So, parents: don't give up on your children. Show them the joy of Christian living, and they will, one day, discover that you had it right all along.

Now as an adult looking back, I am grateful that we had few possessions when we were growing up. Having little in the way of material things forces a young person to begin to think of creative ways to "make it" in the world. Sometimes, when children have everything given to them, they begin to expect it more and appreciate it less. We can easily become lazy and stunted in our growth of maturity. Perhaps we have seen children with so many Christmas and birthday gifts, they can't open them fast enough or remember what they received in the first place. Even at the earliest age, a child can begin to learn that even the best of toys and gifts excites only for a brief time.

The advantage of having little forced my siblings and me to go out and make money on our own. This was the same experience of many past generations. In our earliest years, we were shoveling snow, cutting lawns, delivering newspapers, and even collecting copper and brass to trade in for money.

At thirteen years old, I found a 42-foot brass bar in the middle of the Naugatuck River, likely deposited there from the flood of 1955. I cut it up into small pieces and traded it in for nineteen dollars. In 1973, that was a lot of money for a thirteen-year-old! My older brother made hundreds of dollars collecting copper, scrounging in the Waterbury dump. We even had a small makeshift candy store, where the children from the neighborhood would come to our home and buy candy that we had purchased wholesale. By the time I was sixteen years old, my siblings and I were buying some of our own clothes and many other things.

Often a great work ethic is formed from great financial need, and from that need, an appreciation for the simplest things in life takes shape.

"HERE I AM LORD:" EVEN IN THE SNOW 4

A big day in my life, certainly one of the greatest and a day never to be forgotten—a day when God became real—occurred in the winter of 1973. Early on a Sunday morning, I looked out the window of our second-floor bedroom and saw snow piled up to the bumper of our 1968 Chevy station wagon. We lived in a very small house, but with a 300-foot sloped driveway made of rocks and gravel. Church and Sunday Mass were always an integral part of our life. This day, however, due to the deep snow and a road that had not yet been plowed, I immediately thought to myself, "We are not going to church today."

Next thing I knew, about 6:30 in the morning, my father came into the bedroom, and in his beautiful Irish accent, said to my brothers and me, "C'mon now, boys, it's time to get up. We're going to church." I thought, "Dad, you didn't look out the window — we're not going anywhere." Well, indeed, he had. The next thing I knew, all eight of us, parents and children ranging in age from thirteen to four, walked along our road and then on the highway leading to St. Mary's Church for early morning Mass.

Only one car passed us the entire time. The gentleman stopped and exclaimed, "You people alright?" My father responded, as if it were a beautiful spring day, "We're fine, sir! We're fine, thank you. We're going to church." (Do you remember me writing about life on Fenit Island? Rowing a boat to church? Horse and carriage? Wet and rainy?) For my dad, walking one and a half miles to church in the deep snow was, by comparison, a walk in the park!

Feeling the cold of the morning, I ran ahead of the family and made it to the church first. Upon entering, I immediately felt a warmth in my heart that was well beyond the experience of the welcomed change in temperature. The interior looked stunningly beautiful that day and I had an encounter with God.

There are certain experiences in life that are never forgotten because they are life-transforming. Sometimes they are painful, and sometimes they are beautiful. This one was beautiful. Looking around the church, I quickly realized that, with the exception of two or three elderly women (whom I knew lived right across the street), we were the only family there. Close to the front pew on the right side, all eight of us knelt in a row in the same pew.

With my father kneeling to my immediate right, I turned toward him and looked beyond him to the stained-glass window, and vividly remembered saying to myself, "This is very important to him." At that moment, from the little heart of a twelve-year-old boy came an earnest prayer to God, asking that He be important to me too. God answered that prayer.

Pivotal moments in life are rarely recognized immediately: the chance meeting at a gathering of a future spouse or best friend, a seemingly insignificant business deal that eventually changes the entire direction of a company, career choices that began with random, teenage part-time jobs. One day when I am called home to the Lord, I may have inscribed on the epitaph of my tomb, "God is Big on the Little." That powerful expression came to mind one day during a meditation. Everything in life starts small; nothing starts big. Amazon, Microsoft, and all big corporations begin with an idea.

Waterbury, Connecticut, from where I write, was at one time known as the Brass and Copper Capital of the World. The massive factories—American Brass, Chase, Anaconda—all began small. Someone had an idea, and an amazing city was born.

Sometimes in life we expect big results quickly. This almost never happens. The second step never happens before the first. If we pay attention to the little, and work our best at the small, great results are possible. In the same way, if we disregard the little as insignificant, then the results, too, will be insignificant, and little will be accomplished.

As Scripture states, "For whatever a person sows, that he will also reap" (Galatians 6:7). God desires to bestow gifts upon us. Sometimes we install barriers, perhaps out of fear, or simply because we are too caught up in worldly pursuits and are blind to God's presence. Once the barriers are down, don't be surprised to see the gifts begin to flow.

The greatest gift, the greatest good that can be presented to a child is the gift of faith. Young and old alike, we can all be distracted (sometimes very easily) and quickly find, instead of being a priority, prayer and a life of faith only occur "if I have time." It may be that parents, themselves, never had any encounter with God and therefore don't know what to share.

At all baptisms, I express to parents that if they focus on their own spiritual lives and that of their children, "Your children will thank you forever, and I mean forever." Parents are the first educators of their children, and everyone—at some level—desires the infinite.

Neither my father nor I realized on that snowy Sunday morning, the impact of his decision, and how pivotal it was in my life. Had my father rolled over in bed that day and chosen not to go to church, we would have understood completely—in fact, we expected it. But he didn't. Instead, a very small decision made on that winter morning had powerful repercussions, not only for me, but for my siblings as well. Even my then-four-year old sister still remembers it to this day. God is, indeed, "Big on the Little."

UPON THIS ROCK   5

F ast forward a number of years. My brother and I decided to start a contracting business. It was a knee-jerk, spur of the moment decision on a Saturday morning between two guys in their mid-twenties, essentially over a bowl of Cheerios. At the time, we probably had more brawn than brains, but God can work with passion. We put a $5 ad in a local paper, received six calls for work, purchased a beat-up $1,000 truck, and ultimately, by God's grace, built the company to over 30 employees and approximately fifty subcontractors. God is, indeed, big on the little.

Building with my brother, John (1991)

If all of life's decisions were made when everything was perfectly calculated, lined up, and in place, very little would ever be achieved. The Gospel of Luke 14:31 admonishes us not to go into battle with

10,000 troops when facing an enemy with 20,000 troops. In other words, calculate and be prudent. In more modern-day language, make sure "all your ducks are in a row."

At the same time, the Bible also teaches us to go forward in trust. There are times in life when after prayer and prudent deliberation, the decision to proceed is the wise decision. Not every question needs to be fully answered, and not every negative possibility thoroughly studied. There comes a point with the major decisions in life (work, marriage, career moves, children), that although every question is not yet answered, we have enough prudent information to make the leap in faith. Fear can be stifling and has kept many people from moving forward in life and from achieving hoped-for dreams and aspirations.

Early in our business career, a life-changing event provided a lasting spiritual dimension for our workplace. One day, while putting the finishing touches on a beautiful addition for a customer's home, my brother, John, was working alone. The customer had left, presumably for the entire day. John was now in his mid-twenties and, along with the various secular radio stations he would enjoy listening to, he began to listen to Christian radio.

On this particular day, the homeowner unexpectedly returned home because she had forgotten something, and WIHS Christian radio was playing. As she entered the house, my brother immediately ran across the room and turned it off. Heaven forbid someone would be caught listening to Christian radio! Had he instead been listening to 99 Rock or WTIC Talk radio or WFAN Sports Radio, he would have quite happily kept listening with no change in radio volume.

The piercing words of Scripture cut to the quick of his heart: "Whoever is ashamed of me and of my words, the Son of Man will be ashamed of when he comes in his glory and in the glory of the Father" (Luke 9:26). After she left, John got down on his knees, right in the middle of the living room floor, and prayed silently, "Lord, I am so sorry. I will never do that again." The Apostle Peter denied our Lord, yet he became the rock upon which the Church was built. John, too, sought mercy—and he kept on building.

God can work through everything, and the Lord used that momentary betrayal to turn the heart of my brother to a deeper desire for prayer. As the company grew, there was one particular morning on a jobsite when John asked a number of employees and subcontractors if they would like to start the day with a prayer. The group included Catholics (mainly in name only), a Hindu, and men of no religious affiliation whatsoever. After a momentary awkward silence, almost all said, "Yes."

That began a new chapter at Sullivan Brothers, LLC. A little prayer before each working day became the norm. We then brought prayer into the office three times each day: a brief morning prayer, Angelus at noon, and one decade of the Divine Mercy Chaplet at three o'clock. Perfect? By no means! Phones would be ringing, deliveries arriving, people entering, and the normal day-to-day affairs of any business would be taking place. However, prayer and work (*ora et labora* as the Benedictines say) became a normal part of the workday, just as was cutting lumber, estimating job sites, or swinging a hammer.

Do you pray before work? At work? All too often, people believe that prayer is reserved primarily for church on Sundays and don't think to pray at all during the day. Christ is the Lord of all—work, play, eating, exercise—everything. We can look to the example of St. Teresa of Calcutta, who saw the face of Christ in everyone. Her works of mercy with the poor became her daily prayer. The more we invite Christ into every aspect of our lives, and the more we live in communion with Him, the greater our friendship with the living God emerges. It was prayer that kept our company together.

Many people pray the Morning Offering. The Morning Offering

dedicates the entire day to God. One day, at the beginning of a theology class, a Providence College professor of mine said, "It's not possible to be continually mindful of God at every moment of the day. We have so many other responsibilities that require our focus and attention." The Morning Offering dedicates the entire day to God; our every action, and even our very breath can become a prayer.

The prayer I learned as a child goes something like this: "Oh my Lord, Jesus Christ, I most humbly offer to you all my prayers, works, joys, and sufferings of this day, in union with the Holy Catholic Church throughout the world, in reparation for my sins, for the intentions of the Holy Father [now Pope Francis], especially those intentions of this month, for peace in the world, for the salvation of souls, for the hungry, the poor, the dying, the imprisoned, and for the suffering souls in Purgatory." After that, I would add a few additional, personal petitions. This is my own version of the morning offering. The standard one is slightly different. Church is a house of prayer, but prayer is also meant to be in every house, in every heart, in every day.

FIVE WAYS TO CONVERSION 6

Conversion to a deeper life of faith happens at different times in people's lives. Faith is a gift, of course, open to all. Many find it. Others, for varied reasons, never do. God answers all prayers. Sometimes the answer is yes, and sometimes it is "not yet." The no is only because the Lord knows what we seek may not be for our benefit, or for that of another, at that particular time. God's "no" is sometimes clearly understood later when an unexpected door opens. At other times, we may not understand God's ways until we meet Him in the life to come.

There are prayers, however, to which the answer is always yes and never no, and one of those prayers is the prayer for deeper faith. The prayer for greater faith can certainly be for ourselves. As the Apostles asked, "Lord, increase our faith" (Luke 17:5), so, too, can we. The prayer for greater faith may not necessarily be for ourselves, but for another. St. Monica's prayer for her son, Augustine, bore amazing fruit. In my ten years as a priest, I've discovered that while the greatest request for prayers is for bodily health (for self or another), the second greatest is for the faith life of another, usually children and grandchildren. Hope, with Divine hope, that prayers for the faith life of another will be answered, but also have peace that although desired, you may not live to see it. The grace may come after you are called home to the Lord.

For others, faith may have been present as a child, but for different reasons, it is diminished or even lost in the high school or college years. In the Gospel of Matthew we read the Parable of the Sower: "Some seed fell on rocky places, where it did not have much soil. It sprang up quickly because the soil was shallow. But when the sun came up, the plants were scorched and withered, because they had no roots" (Matthew 13:5-6).

This book is essentially a book about conversion, whether that conversion comes gradually, suddenly, or by some combination of the two. Whatever vocation we have chosen, there needs to be a continual call to deeper conversion. Once we believe that we have "made it" or that we've "done enough," we are actually at a very low place spiritually. Love has no limit, but we often place limits on how much we are willing to love. As said previously, stagnancy is poison to the spiritual life, and there is always a higher place of love to be revealed and experienced. One of the greatest joys of the priesthood is to witness this conversion — a change of heart. Perhaps more than any other vocation in the world, those called to priesthood not only witness changed hearts, but are often the catalyst for that change.

Conversion and a change of heart to Christ essentially come in five forms. There are more than five, of course. God, who is Infinite Love, is not limited and reveals Himself to us in a multitude of ways, yet these five, I believe, are the most common. One experience that is shared by every changed heart is an encounter with the Living God. This encounter is real. It is intimate. It is an experience of profound love.

The first is the rarest. It is **intellectual conversion**, whereby a person comes to a life of faith through study, reading, catechism, or dogma. St. Augustine of Hippo, once steeped in a life of sin and earthly pride, experienced a great intellectual conversion primarily through the teachings of spiritual giants like St. Ambrose. The mind, by God's grace, is enlightened. The "light," so to speak, is turned on, and we see clearly, perhaps for the first time. Although it is somewhat rare for people to "read" their way into a life of faith, when it does happen, the many arguments and proof texts that defended our once-formed positions of resistance simply disappear. For some, this change is rapid; for others, it occurs over extended periods. Usually, something significant happens before catechism. An unrealized grace is already stirring.

There is no right or wrong way to come to God. The Lord knows us much better than we know ourselves. He uses our gifts, habits, and —yes— even our weaknesses and faults, to reveal Himself. Those who find God strictly through books and learning are, in the whole scheme of things, few. It is said that the longest distance that the Christian will ever travel is eighteen inches — from the head to the heart. While it is true that the majority of conversions are first a conversion of heart (which then leads to a deeper desire to know God), a change of heart for some (usually very intelligent people) begins in the head.

The second form of conversion to Christ flows from the **preached word.** The Bible says, "Faith comes from hearing, and hearing the Word of God" (Romans 10:17). "The word of God is sharper than any double-edged sword; it penetrates even to divide soul and spirit, joints and marrow; it judges the thoughts and attitudes of the heart" (Hebrews 4:12). The preached word is meant to inspire, console, and fill the heart with joy. At the same time, it is meant to give comfort to the sorrowing. The Scriptures are not "dead words" from thousands of years ago; rather, they are timeless, and they speak to the heart in every age and time.

The human heart has not changed. We are created in a certain way by God. We are broken and flawed, while at the same time, made for greatness. Our surroundings have changed, and the world is most certainly a much different place than it was when our parents and grandparents lived. In spite of a world that looks much different from the past, the human heart will always seek happiness, will know pain, joy, the effects of sin, and the happiness that comes from living virtuously. The preached word seeks to penetrate them all, touching the heart at every moment of life. My homiletics professor, a priest by the name of Fr. John Rowan, said in class, "The purpose of the homily is to move the faithful to prayer and repentance. The homily fails if it does not move the people to action."

Scripture is not a collection of meaningless words, although sometimes the preacher can present it as if it were. In his early writings, Pope Francis speaks about homilies that are not well prepared or inspiring. Not all preachers possess the same level of gift, yet studies show that only fifteen percent of preaching is words. If that is the case, what is the remaining eighty five percent? What leads to an inspiring homily is often not the fifteen percent, but the eighty five percent —passion, posture, eye contact, intonation, voice quality, and perhaps above all, the priest's prayer life. If a priest is not alive in Christ, his words will eventually be accurately perceived as dead. A prayerless homily can fool people for only so long. The true depth of the preacher is eventually revealed. In the same way, if the preached word is inspired by Christ through time spent in prayer and preparation, that word will change hearts, lives, families, and yes, even society itself.

The people of God deserve our best. If they are to be awakened by the spoken word, those of us who are priests and pastors must strive to feed our flocks as best we can. There is little worse than a dead, boring, uninspiring homily. The two wings of the Mass, so to speak, the Liturgy of the Word, and the Liturgy of the Eucharist, are both meant to feed. If one or the other is lacking, the Mass will be an uninspiring experience and can often lead a parish into a crash landing. Priests have a great responsibility to continually seek God's grace to be full of the Holy Spirit, and to spend themselves feeding hungry souls.

Another very important form of 'preaching' is listening. If a priest has a welcoming heart, people will seek his counsel. Most counsel is simply listening, showing people you care for them and giving them your time. Most people in a hospital bed will not remember what you said, but they will remember that "the priest was there." People don't remember how "professional" a priest is, or his "pastoral techniques," but they will remember his heart. There are priests who rarely, if ever, have a person call to make an appointment. Perhaps his own fears, weaknesses, or struggles (maybe even his own selfishness of time) is like a large billboard across his chest that reads, "I'm not available." This is a great loss to the people of God, because the loss of even one sheep can have a ripple effect across generations. In the same way, a soul changed and transformed is like the possessed man, (Mark 5:1-20), the blind man, (John 9:6), and the hemorrhaging woman, (Mark 5:25-34) who after being healed by Jesus, desire nothing more than to share the joyous news with everyone.

The preached word is not only from the pulpit, as most would believe. The priest's word is more often heart-to-heart, one soul at a time. Both modes of connection are important, both inspire, and both grow a parish. Along with face-to-face meetings and counseling, one of the greatest means of encountering parishioners is simply to stand outside after Mass, shaking hands, blessing religious objects, or listening to people's concerns while intently looking them in the eye with affection. Children, too, sense this love and feel welcomed, and for that reason, want to be near the priest. This is called the "ministry of presence," and what it does more than anything else is make Christ present. It often happens that so many people want to talk, it can sometimes take an additional two hours after the last Mass before the priest is able to return to the rectory. This is time well spent. In fact, it essentially becomes a two-hour homily, often more effective than anything preached from the ambo.

Mother Teresa once said, "Never worry about numbers. Help one person at a time and always start with the person nearest you."

The third means of conversion begins with a **profound realization**

of the "beautiful" and a desire to seek the source of that beauty. When we see something beautiful, we want to know its source—from where it came. We desire more, to be filled to the brim. Both Pope Benedict, and in more recent years, Bishop Robert Barron of Minnesota, have spoken extensively on beauty. The beauty of God, creation, art, architecture—the list goes on. It is very often the beautiful that first inspires a soul to go deeper, to seek more. Even the greatest unbeliever will appreciate beauty: the beauty of a joyful person, the beauty of an early morning sunrise, the crashing of waves, inspiring church architecture, or classical art of centuries past. All of these inspire and can draw us deeper into taking the first step towards God—a beauty so deep that the heart is drawn to the deeper reality of Beauty Itself.

A powerful and joyful experience for both parents and priests is often witnessed at the sacraments of baptism and marriage. As water is poured over the forehead of an innocent child at baptism, invoking the Father, Son, and Holy Spirit, tears of joy often emerge from parents, godparents, and friends—and, yes, even the priest. Joy is at the heart of who God is, and when we experience these moments of great joy and beauty, God is revealed. Weddings, being an occasion of great joy (Christ's first miracle was at the wedding of Cana in Galilee, John 2:1—11), also provide a tremendous means of encountering God. As stated previously, it takes three to marry: the man, woman, and Christ. If a church full of guests at a wedding can witness the beauty of this sacramental covenant, they may begin to ask themselves, "Why would I want to get married on a beach? Why by a justice of the peace? Could it be that marriage in a sacred place has so much more to offer than any other venue?"

Beauty can penetrate the darkest places. A person can be so steeped in sin that there seems to be no limit to this darkness. It becomes in our life like an all-absorbing black hole that pulls the very heart and soul out of a person. Conversely, the beautiful also has no limit. We will never take in or acquire all of God. As St. Augustine said many centuries ago in his famous Confessions: "You breathed your fragrance on me. I drew in my breath and now I pant for you. I have tasted you: and now I hunger and thirst for more." The 'more' that we all seek will never come from this world. Both the beauty of creation (our material world) and that of the soul—these two great beauties that God has graciously bestowed on the world—are sometimes the smallest of seeds that inspire the heart to seek God for the first time. Once the heart finds God, there is no end to the riches borne of this great treasure.

A majestic Christmas at the Basilica (2022)

Every person, including the unbeliever, is attracted to the beautiful. Beauty raises us up from the mundane and mediocre and stirs a soul to desire more. When the eyes of the soul experience beauty in any of its forms, the soul lifts us up to a higher plateau. Sin, in all of its deceptive forms, is ugly, and as we all know from our own experiences, we all go to that ugly place from time to time. Beauty trumps and crushes the ugliness of sin and selfishness, and it inspires our innermost desire to be more, to live for more—the ultimate "more" being life with Christ.

Within this same category of beauty can be placed the beauty of another person. Joy, kindness, charity, patience, and love exemplified in the heart and life of another may very well be the only "bible" ever witnessed. Beautiful landscapes, sunrises, ocean waves, or a newborn child—all mentioned above—may provide the initial spark and seed of desire. Yet, it is the lived reality and experience of seeing Christ in another that will surpass them all.

We can preach Christ "until the cows come home," but if we never see His beauty shining forth in another person, then faith may be initiated, but not deepened, and therefore less beautiful. The human person is created not to be an island, but to live in relationship with another. What a gift and privilege it is to be Christ to another. "This little light of mine, I'm going to let it shine," sung by countless little children, is true for all ages. "Let your light shine before men, that they may see the good that you do, and give glory to God" (Matthew 5:16).

A fourth means of conversion is, perhaps, the most mysterious of all. It is a change of heart through **tragedy**. It happens that tragedy and the deepest pains of life can draw a person closer to God, sometimes for the first time. Tragedy causes some to lose faith, but others to return or to hold on tighter, to seek comfort in their loss. Tragedy, suffering, and death cause us to ask the deeper questions of life. "Why? What? How?" A person, instead of letting go of God, sometimes runs to God; people need Someone to hold on to, to comfort them, to give them hope for tomorrow.

Priests find funerals to be an incredible means of evangelization. Many priests prefer to celebrate funerals over weddings. Death can remind us of our own mortality and lead us to take inventory of the direction of our own lives. At essentially every funeral, some in attendance are crossing the threshold of a church for the first time in a long time (perhaps for the first time ever) and are surprisingly open to hearing about God. They may enter simply with the desire to comfort and to be present to family and friends, but leave having their own experience of God—an experience that may be the first of many.

Very often at funerals, I include words in the homily that are especially meant for those who may be of minimal faith by saying, "If your loved one could speak to us right now after meeting the Lord they would probably say, 'Love deeper. Be faithful. Seek God.' They may end by crying out loudly, 'It's worth it!'" In the words of the Mass, there is a hope-filled Preface prayer: "Life is changed, not ended." This is a most beautiful Christian belief, and it gives us hope that this life is not all there is. We are often tempted to live as if it is. St. Paul, in his letter to the Corinthians, wrote, "Eye has not seen, ear has not heard, nor has it so much entered the heart of man what God has prepared for those who love him" (1 Corinthians 2:9).

There is not a church on the face of the earth that promotes the Communion of Saints, the Family of God, more than the Catholic Church does. In many churches, older ones in particular, painted on the walls of the sanctuary, or etched in stained glass, are images of the saints—those who have gone before us. At the Mass, the entire Church is present: the Church Triumphant (those in Heaven), the Church Suffering (those in Purgatory when a period of cleansing and purification is needed), and the Church Militant (those now living on earth, including those in the pew). For those already with the Lord, they are actually more alive now than they ever were in this world, because they are with the source of Life and Love Itself, Christ Jesus. This reality gives us great peace.

Tragedy is experienced not only at death but also in life. Unexpected accidents, medical emergencies, financial loss, family betrayal, sins of self or another can cause us in the same way as does death, to run toward or away from God. Living through the experience of tragedy, we can often feel like there is no answer, no way out, no future light. We may even try to numb ourselves, our feelings, by escaping into behaviors that end up hurting us even more. In our pain and darkness, we often try to find worldly solace in places where it does not exist or, at best, exists barely and only temporarily. The "band-aid," whatever that is, will eventually peel away. It is then that the wound is again exposed, and hopefully at that time, the door of our future faith life is opened to allow the Divine Healer to enter.

Allowing Christ to enter into our pain is a great first step. "The Doctor is in" —the Divine Doctor—who all too well knows suffering and pain. Christ bore our sins and our pain on the cross. We know from Sacred Scripture that every human person will, in one way or another in life, have a cross to bear. If we had a choice, we would, as Fr. Benedict Groeschel once said, very likely choose a Styrofoam cross with a little wheel at the lower end. The answer to the "why" of our sufferings and tragedies may not be revealed in this life, yet we will one day know their deeper and mysterious meaning. In the meantime, as best we can, we have to trust that there is an answer and that God knows what it is. Running to and embracing God in tragedy is, in itself, painful, but in Him alone lies our peace and consolation.

Those who live with good health (both bodily and spiritually) and have not as yet in their life experienced tragedy, rarely conceptualize what it must be like to live in sorrow or pain day after day. Ideally, as we mature in faith, hope and love, we are able to offer our suffering to God, so as to be configured to Christ's own suffering. We may have heard it said from our mothers when we were children, "Offer it up."

This is, of course, easier said than done. It is the mature soul that is able to do so—sometimes even with joy. A modern-day saint who exemplified such joy in suffering was St. Maximillian Kolbe, who offered his life in place of a husband and father at Auschwitz. He willingly suffered starvation and lethal injection out of love for another. This is a much deeper spirituality and requires great grace. When suffering is offered to God, it begins the making of a saint.

The fifth and last means to conversion to Christ often occurs in later years, in the maturing of life and quite simply is related to the **reality of death**. We begin to realize as we age, that we are closer to the tomb than we are to the womb, and thoughts of the reality of our own mortality begin to enter our mind. At these later stages in life, it is common for a person to think about the question, "What will happen next?" and to begin an inventory of life. My father was always a very devout man, but after his retirement, he was able to attend Church a little more than simply on Sundays. A fellow parishioner said to him, "Hey, Sully, I see you're here at Church quite a bit more now." Without skipping a beat and with characteristic humor, my father quickly replied, "I'm cramming for the finals!" On that final day—the day of our last breath, whenever it comes—we need, as best we can, to be prepared. The Bible says, "We know not the day nor the hour" (Matthew 25:13) and to "keep watch" (Matthew 24:42). The Irish comedian, Hal Roach, once said, "Live every day as if it was your last, and one day you'll be right!" There comes a point when many people begin to realize on the day when they are called home, that they don't want to meet a stranger when they meet the Lord Jesus and perhaps even hear the words, "I never knew you" (Matthew 7:21-23).

I have found in my ten years of priesthood that a number of people, as they approach the autumn years of their life, whether believers or non-believers, desire to meet with a priest and have a "life" confession. I strongly encourage this, especially for those for whom the Sacrament of Reconciliation was not a normal practice in their lives. As we approach our final years, we can look back and review not only the good that we have done, but also those things we have done that have hurt ourselves or others. The next chapter is dedicated to this healing Sacrament. Expressing the words, "I'm sorry," in the presence of another person (namely, the priest), who acts in the person of Christ, despite how difficult it may be, is always a moment of profound healing. Moreover, it peacefully prepares us for our end.

Fear, although not the best of motivators, sometimes does move us to action. People are not so much afraid of death itself as they are of the process of dying. Will it be a long illness? Will I be a burden to my family and loved ones? Will I be in pain? Every priest, in all our visits to the sick and homebound, knows that in the heart of every sick and dying person is the deepest, most poignant question of all: "Will I be saved?" God has a name and that name is Mercy. We trust in His merciful love to save us.

BROKEN BUTTERFLY 7

Absolutely central to any conversion to Christ is sorrow: sorrow for the things I've done, sorrow for the things I didn't do but should have done, sorrow for bad decisions that affected and hurt others, sorrow for destructive behaviors, sorrow for my selfishness, and sorrow for offending God. There is a line from a once popular 1970s' novel, Love Story, that says "Love is never having to say you're sorry." These are terribly fallacious words with the exact opposite being eminently true. True love desires never to offend, yet when we do, sorrow for offending the ones we love (and even those we don't particularly care for), should as best we can, be readily spoken. The two most difficult words the human person will ever speak are, "I'm sorry." Speaking these two sometimes painful, yet healing words expresses humility and meekness. Some people, in arrogance, are unable or unwilling to speak them.

Humility is not the greatest virtue; love (charity) is. In St. Paul's First Letter to the Corinthians, he writes, "Faith, hope, and love remain, these three; and the greatest of these is love" (1 Corinthians 13:13). Humility is rather the foundational virtue from which all other virtues build upon and grow. In other words, without humility, a person will not grow in his/her spiritual life. The word humility comes from the Latin word, "*humus*," which means "earth." A person who is "down to earth" is one who is practical, realistic, unpretentious, and living without illusions.

Some people confuse humility with needing to possess a poor self-image. This is not humility. There is, however, such a thing as a false humility. An example of this is when people receive a compliment for something done well, and their response is self-deprecating. Humility is about the truth of a person, therefore the appropriate response to a sincere and truthful compliment, rather than being disingenuous, is simply to say, "Thank you." A humble person can recognize his/her gifts and talents as gifts from God and be thankful for them. If someone complimented Michael Jordan as one of the greatest basketball players who ever lived, his appropriate response would be a sincere "Thank you." He would know this fact, this truth about himself, simply based on the statistics from his years of play.

Humility is foundational to being able to express the words, 'I'm sorry." Some people are unable to say them. They are always right and never wrong. It is always someone else's fault. Perhaps we know someone like this; perhaps we are a little like this ourselves? Many years ago, while on a jobsite, a woman (the homeowner) made a significant mistake in relation to a necessary communication concerning her job. She said to me, "I'm sorry," but admitted some days later when the job was complete that it was the first time she had spoken those words in many decades. Her father had told her when she was a young teenage girl, never to say those words, as they were a sign of weakness.

Every conversion to Christ involves an, "I'm sorry:" a fundamental realization that my life needs to change and begin in a new direction. This realization is freeing, and this new awareness is life-giving. Unapologetic attitudes, always needing to be right, and always needing to win or "one up" the other choke a person, locking them in a darkened cocoon. Like the butterfly who finally breaks free, the words "I'm sorry" break open the darkened heart, and with that, comes the happy realization that a new and brighter horizon is attainable and awaits us.

The "I'm sorry's" just discussed are meant both for another person and for God. Expressing these words to another person can be exceedingly difficult because it involves great vulnerability. How will the other person receive it? Will the phone hang up? Will the text or email be ignored? The letter never answered? The door slammed in my face?

These are all possibilities and legitimate concerns, because with the words "I'm sorry" comes the possibility of rejection. This being said, if/when we come to a point in life when we realize that we have offended and wronged another, we need to take the risk of potential rejection and "make the call."

Most people, when they truly convey a heartfelt apology to another, are happy they did so, even if their apology is rejected. We would be pleasantly surprised at how often words of apology are welcomed, because at the core of our being, we know well the interior pain that unforgiveness brings. Words of sorrow are often reciprocated, and it is then that both people are set free. Hopefully it is the Christian, in imitation of Christ, who is able to make the first move and rise above those many interior voices that keep reminding us, "They should apologize first! I will when they will!" How often a priest witnesses broken and hurtful relationships taken to the grave. Some injuries, indeed, are admittedly serious; others could have been easily resolved decades ago.

Expressing sorrow to a person is one thing. Expressing sorrow to God—quite another. I don't believe there is a person anywhere who would disagree with the fact that the former apology is much harder to make than the latter. God always desires to forgive; human beings sometimes do. God's name is Mercy, and the Lord continually invites all of humanity not only to receive mercy, but to show mercy to others. Christ never rejects the repentant sinner: "The humble, contrite heart, oh God, you will not spurn" (Psalm 51).

In the Catholic faith, we have a beautiful practice, a sacrament called Confession or Reconciliation. As Catholics, we believe that with the confession of sin to a priest comes a profound grace to help and strengthen us to conquer whatever vice it is with which we are struggling. The Sacrament of Reconciliation is backed by Sacred Scripture. After the Resurrection, when Christ appears in the upper room, He says to His disciples (who are the first priests), "Whose sins you shall forgive, they are forgiven them, whose sins you shall retain, they are retained" (John 20:23). The forgiving and retaining of sin that Jesus speaks of presumes the verbal telling of the sin. The Letter of James says, "Confess your sins one to another and pray for one another that you may be healed" (5:16). From the early Church, this was understood to be in the context of the priesthood.

Practically speaking, the vast majority of Catholics who have experienced the healing grace that flows from the Sacrament find it a beautiful, freeing experience. As a priest, I too go to confession approximately once each month. In fact, the best confessors are those who also frequent the Sacrament themselves and know first-hand its healing power. I compare the confession of sin to a shower that most people take daily to clean the outside of their bodies. Confession of sin is a spiritual 'shower' that cleans the inside. Both are beneficial; in fact, both are needed. After a short period of time, one would say of the unclean, unwashed body, the very words Martha spoke to the Lord concerning her dead brother Lazarus, "Surely, Lord, there will be a stench" (John 11:39). Our experiences of personal sin and/or the sins of another allow us to know all too well those same words concerning our soul: "Surely Lord, there is a stench." The body is cleaned with soap and water and shampoo. In the Sacrament of Confession, we are cleaned with grace and peace and Divine Life.

At the advent of Protestantism in the 16th century, the practice of Sacramental confession was abandoned by the Reformers with the thought being that a priest was not needed. Instead, they believed it was sufficient to confess directly to Christ. Over time, especially in more recent decades, this same thinking has creeped into the Catholic Church as well, with many Catholics not having gone to the Sacrament perhaps for many decades. People truly do not know the beauty that they are missing. In response to the thinking of our Protestant brothers and sisters, Catholics agree that we, too, should go directly to Christ with our sins. In fact, there is a beautiful ancient practice within the church of examining one's conscience at the end of each day, asking God for the grace to begin tomorrow anew. In Catholic thought, this is not a case of either/or (God *or* priest), but rather a case of both/and (God *and* priest). Scripture indicates both, and our own human experience echoes the beauty and necessity of that reality.

In a world that is truly blinded to the reality of what sin is, countless people never go to confession, because they truly believe they have nothing to confess; they do nothing wrong. The power of evil—the devil—camouflages sin and blinds us to its reality, preventing us from recognizing it in our own lives. If sin is not believed or recognized, then conversion is not needed. The more a person falls in love with Christ, the more he or she will recognize true holiness and thus, the stench of sin.

The greatest reason, I believe, for a person's avoidance of the Sacrament of Reconciliation is fear. Speaking those two most difficult words previously discussed, "I'm sorry," to another human person, namely the priest, is far from easy. I have been going to Confession all my life, and as much as the experience is like no other, there is still that part of human pride and weakness that doesn't want to admit to wrongdoing. Along with the two most difficult words are the six words that begin every confession, "Bless me Father, I have sinned." The fear is a fear of being exposed, fear of being found out, fear that another human person will know my weakness, that perhaps what has been hidden in the dark closet has now come into the light and someone else knows it. Priests, by the way, have an amazing gift of forgetfulness. The most confessions I've ever heard in one day was close to 100, and believe me, just like Christ forgets our sin, so does the priest.

The priest acts in *persona Christi,* in the person of Christ. The penitent is confessing to Christ with the priest acting in His person. Through the words of the priest (the words of absolution), which are the words of the Church, grace is imparted. These healing words are worth expressing here. *"God the Father of mercies, through the death and resurrection of his Son, has reconciled the world to himself and poured out the Holy Spirit for the forgiveness of sins; through the ministry of the Church may God grant you pardon and peace, and I absolve you from your sins in the name of the Father and of the Son and of the Holy Spirit."* Without fail, a person leaving the confessional after hearing those healing, grace-filled words, experiences the relief of a burden lifted. The sin has been spoken and is now wiped away.

As a priest, I have witnessed this, heard this, countless times. Penitents have said that after leaving the confessional, they even feel lighter in their bodies. Sin is, indeed, a burden by which we become enslaved, and because we are a body and a spirit (not *just* a body and not *just* a spirit, rather both), it makes perfect sense that the alleviated burden of the soul affects our very body too. The human person is not an angel; we speak and we touch and we experience. The healing voice of the priest breathes out the healing words of Christ, and these words *speak* to our deepest needs and *touch* our darkest places where we experience His loving voice. We are again made free from sin and when we *experience* the freedom of forgiveness, deeper conversion is desired, because we quickly realize that forgiveness makes us happy.

Do not be afraid of confessing your sins. If it has been a long time, perhaps make an appointment to talk to a priest, to sit down and review your entire life. These "Life Confessions" generally take between 30 and 60 minutes. There are almost always tears; first tears of sorrow—of repentance—but at the end, without fail, tears of joy, relief, and interior peace. That is what forgiveness does. Speaking those two most difficult words, "I'm sorry," suddenly places a person on the fast track to God, because he/she has broken through the barrier that enslaves: the obstacle that is sin. We get excited about getting up again and starting anew, this time with a greater resolve to be better and live better for Christ and neighbor. The experience of forgiveness creates in the heart of the penitent an ability and even a desire to speak those two words again (the next time is easier) and then leads us to speak the three most beautiful words, "*I love You*. I love the world You created, Lord. I love myself despite my faults and failings. I love my family and will strive to love my neighbor as myself. I love You, Lord. Change and convert my heart."

ALWAYS MORE OF THAT   8

Every person, no matter what his or her calling in life, ultimately desires to love and be loved. Love has no limit. Without love, life is empty and meaningless. With love, even in the midst of struggles, love sustains and brings about interior solace.

The love of God can never be fully exhausted in this life. There is always another rung on the spiritual ladder and always more and greater possibilities for love. The "more" of a person is profoundly deep. The "more" of God is infinitely greater. There is, in this life, (again due to our weakened nature), a tendency to fall into the trap of doing that which is least. "What is the least I can do and still get to Heaven?" "What is the least of my time and resources that I can give to others or to my Church?" "What is the least I can do at work and still expect a raise and promotion?" "What is the least I can do at school and still get a great grade?" "What parish has a Mass that is ten minutes quicker than the one I go to?" "Do I really need to go the extra mile?" "How far can I go before crossing the line into serious sin?" Least! Least! Least!

How about the best?! Do we ever ask that question in regard to spiritual things? "What is the best of myself that I can give?" "How can I most help others with the gifts that God has given me?" The popular prayer of St. Francis, "It is in giving that we receive," rings true in the heart of every human person, yet we are drawn to live otherwise. The Second Vatican Council, addressing the heart of the human person says, "Man can only fully discover his true self in a sincere giving of himself" (Vatican II, *Gaudium et spes*, 24).

If we are always looking for the least, we'll never grow in our relationship with God (or for that matter with any person). This is a tragedy, because the human person is meant to grow. Stagnancy is a poison to spiritual life. If we are not growing in our relationship with God, we are actually diminishing, because with the passage of time and age, greater love and wisdom should emerge, not less. If we love God the same at age eighty as we did at sixty, as we did at forty-five, as we did as a teenager, that would be a shame. I always express to our wedding couples that I hope their wedding day is not the happiest day of their lives. How many couples, brides in particular, say that their wedding day will be the "happiest day of my life?" Imagine if it were! Everything downhill after that? The best has already been experienced? With Christ in our life, the best is always yet to come. Love is meant to grow. Indeed, couples can love each other (and God) more after fifty years of marriage than they did on their wedding day and during their younger years. Like the burning bush in Exodus 3, when a person loves deeply, we are never consumed, but rather like Moses, our "eyes are undimmed and our strength unabated" (Deuteronomy 34:7).

A Benedictine monk once said to me, "If God is pure act and if we are to imitate God, then we too must act." When we do, we experience in both our prayer and actions more and more of the living God. If we do not act, we will find ourselves falling into the chasm of stagnancy, which slowly erodes and brings death to the soul. When we live a life of indifference and mediocrity for things spiritual, we begin to lose sense of our deepest meaning and purpose for living.

When in Ireland, shortly after my ordination, I had the privilege of staying in the same parish rectory where my father grew up. What a joy it was to celebrate Mass at the very altar, and touch the very font where he was baptized!

**Baptismal font,
Church of the Purification**

    The priest there was a delightful man, and we enjoyed each other's company. He did, however, say something that disturbed me and that I will never forget: "A good priest," he said, "is a fast priest." He meant, of course, the priest who celebrates a fast Mass. He then added, admittedly meaning to be humorous, "Start coming up from the genuflection before you go down." In other words, you'll save a second.

    Sunday Mass was less than a half hour. What a shame! The attitude "I'm here to get out of here" will never lift a person to a higher place. My father used to say, "They can't wait to get out of here, to get home to what they weren't doing." If we want our faith fast and cheap, we will "get what we pay for." That being said, the priest has a great

Always More Of That

responsibility (according to his gifts) to give to the people that which will inspire. If a priest is unprepared, uninspiring, and the music is bad, what can be expected from the people? Excitement? Hardly!

Enthusiasm breeds enthusiasm, and success breeds success. People want to be a part of something that is alive and life-giving, otherwise they will be looking at their watches and thinking of the afternoon game or dinner engagement. If a priest, for whatever reason, is not alive in Christ, parishioners cannot be entirely blamed for lacking in faith. If the priest is lively, prayerful, and joyful—the parish will grow. If not, it very likely won't. Reverence for the Mass and Eucharist and preaching (as best he can according to his gifts), along with quality music, all contribute to a beautiful liturgy. People will not say, "When will all this be over?" Rather, they will say things like, "I didn't want it to stop!" or "I really felt like I was in Church today."

This being said, people also have a responsibility to prepare for Mass. How often it is said, "I get nothing out of it." The question can then be asked, "What have you put *into* it?" Have you prayerfully prepared? Perhaps read the scriptures prior to coming to church? Church is not a sacramental "car wash" as Dr. Scott Hahn one quipped. We must not enter the church and then expect to be "sprayed" with grace as we come out the other end, while having been in "park" the whole time. The priest is not an entertainer; he is a minister of the Divine.

Not every experience of Mass will be the same. There are times we may enter church feeling lonely or sad and the priest is preaching about the joy of the Gospel. At other times, we may be filled with the joy of a recent engagement or baptism, and the priest may be preaching about death and sin. No matter what we are feeling when entering church, we can find solace in the fact that we were "there", that we gave God our time.

In the same way that we may not feel fulfilled at Mass, there are days when we simply do not feel like going to work or doing something that our spouse or loved one needs. Yet we do it anyway. In fact, we all have responsibilities and simply must rise above what we are feeling at a particular moment and do what needs to be done according to our state in life. Perhaps we have heard the expression, "Eighty percent of success is just showing up." We are often tempted not to show up and instead to live selfishly with our time and energies. When we "show up" for God, we can be assured, despite our "feelings" at Mass, whatever they are, that God is present. He desires to shed His grace upon a soul open to receiving Him.

One of the most common reasons or excuses used for not attending Mass or living a life of prayer and devotion is, "I'm too busy." Mother Theresa once said, "If we are too busy for God, then we are just too busy." Perhaps B.U.S.Y. is an appropriate acronym for "**B**eing **U**nder **S**atan's **Y**oke." The power of evil that exists in the world distracts us continually with the many activities that consume our time from that which is most important, namely living in relationship with God. Our busy lives and schedules can eventually preoccupy our time so much that before we know it, our lives have little prayer, little church – little God. A much better acronym to live by while using the same four letters is "**B**uilding **U**p **S**trength in **Y**ou." *That* is what living close to Jesus does for us.

There are two attitudes a person can have at the beginning of each day: "I get to get up," or "I've got to get up." In more spiritual language, once preached by Archbishop Fulton Sheen, "Good morning, God," or, "Good God, morning!" With Christ at the center of our life, through the joys and sufferings, we are able to say, "Good morning, God! I get to get up today." Wouldn't it be amazing if every Catholic, in every village, town, and city, could get up on a Sunday morning and exclaim, "Good morning, God! I get to go to Church today!"

Many of us who are now a bit older, from time to time (or perhaps even more often than that), think of our younger years with a sense of nostalgia, as that time in life when things were more innocent and less complicated. We were also stronger, more agile and in most cases, healthier than in our older years. Some may even desire to turn the life clock back again to Jack Benny's eternal thirty-nine, if not earlier. Those in their eighties may desire to experience their sixties again, those in their sixties to relive their forties or fifties, and so on. Ah, we may think, "Those were the good old days!"

For some, hopefully most, our younger years really were special and joy-filled times. As children we were happy: we played, had loving parents and laughed, felt loved and secure. If there were problems and struggles (every life has them) they were often hidden from our eyes. We were protected from early hurt and pain and we grew up (at least in our earliest years) thinking this is the way life is meant to be.

As we grow and mature, we begin to realize that the world is not always kind and people are not always good. Loving and even living can be difficult. Perhaps in our twenties or thirties or later, although our childhood may have been pleasant, tragedy can strike in one form or another: a relationship once precious is no longer, finances once plentiful have disappeared, health once enjoyed is overtaken by sickness and a hoped-for loving family replaced with abuse and dysfunction. Yes, sometimes the passage of time is less than kind and good, and a life that hoped for love sadly shifts to mere survival.

The body declines and weakens over time. We are not in the garden of Eden, and in this beautiful but fallen world, that is simply the way it is. While the body declines, God has blessed the heart with the ability to continue to expand. We reach our peak physical strength somewhere around the age of twenty-five. We reach our peak cardio-vascular strength somewhere around the age of thirty-seven. After these years, we can't run as fast, throw as hard, or jump as high as we were once able to. The natural progression of life, and of the body, is one of weakening. Isn't it interesting that Christ died and rose between those two strong ages, the age of thirty-three?

While the body weakens, the spirit is not meant to. A person can be ninety-five years old, filled with cancer, weighing ninety pounds, and can still be growing spiritually. There is, indeed, no limit to love. The reason we desire to live a long life is not to see how many medications we can store in our medicine cabinets or how frequently or infrequently we can make our doctor's appointments. No, the reason we want to live a long life is because we know in the very core of our being that there is a greater capacity to love. There is always more to be had, and as a result, more to give. We ultimately desire to experience this greater love until the day we are called home to Love Itself.

"IS THIS NOT THE CARPENTER'S SON?"

9

Work is a blessing, although in reality, it began as a curse. In the book of Genesis—the first book of the Bible — God says, "By the sweat of your brow, you shall eat bread" (Genesis 3:19). Work is now required and necessary for man to survive. But even in our fallen and rebellious state, God loves us so much that he attaches not only satisfaction to work, but sanctification. We can, through our work (our vocation), experience the love of the living God. The word "vocation" applies to every form of calling, every type of work. Often, when people hear the word "vocation," they instinctively think only of priesthood and religious life. The word "vocation" comes from the Latin word "*vocare*," meaning "to call." Every person has a calling from God, a mission in life to serve, and through this call, to discover that a life lived for others is the only way a person will find true joy. *Gaudium et spes* is worth quoting again: "Man can only fully discover his true self in a sincere giving of himself."

Many people believe they come close to God only in prayer, in church, reading the Bible, singing spiritual hymns, or serving in a soup kitchen. While all of these are certainly true and beautiful, our calling (our daily work) is a road, even a "highway," to God, and indeed our work can be a prayer of praise. In 1981, Pope St. John Paul II wrote a beautiful encyclical entitled "Through Work" (*Laborem Exercens*). In it, he writes that work is defined as "any activity by man, whether manual or intellectual, that can and must be recognized as work." Work is one of the characteristics that distinguishes man from the rest of creation.

If I may for a moment speak of physical labor, this type of work was so dear to my heart for the twenty-five years of my adult life preceding priesthood. Christ, too, was a carpenter. St. Joseph was a carpenter. This particular trade, 2,000 years ago, would have encompassed much more than just wood, and it likely included stone work as well.

The trades today, although so different from years ago, are still very noble professions. Carpenters, plumbers, electricians, HVAC technicians, stone workers, toolmakers, mechanics, and landscapers all imitate Christ in that they employ their hands — and in different ways, they create, build, and beautify. With the advent of computers in more recent decades, fewer men are entering into professions that involve manual labor.

In the United States today, many of the tradespeople are foreign born: immigrants from Poland, Albania, Mexico, Brazil, Columbia, Ireland. It is often hard to find American-born men entering the trades. In fact, it has been said that for every five people retiring from the trades, only three are entering. These immigrants are hard workers seeking a better life, and they are not afraid to work long hours.

Some people view the trades that involve physical labor as less honorable than the more high-paying or "prestigious" careers, and the trades are often looked upon as somewhat demeaning. This perception needs to change. It is manual labor that built everything in this country: homes, businesses, bridges, roads, machinery. It is the hands of hard-working tradespeople that create and build. As the bumper sticker on the back of a pickup truck referring to Jesus proudly reads, "My boss is a Jewish carpenter."

**Renovation of Blessed Sacrament Church,
Waterbury, Conn. (2005)**

A few months before entering seminary, while still working daily in the business world, I was at a gathering of priests and deacons. Word had gotten out that I would soon be entering seminary to become a priest. While at this gathering, within earshot of a priest who was talking to others, I heard him say of me in a somewhat derogatory way, "He's a contractor." In other words, "Don't expect too much." Much was not expected of Jesus either. "Is this not the carpenter's son?" (Matthew 15:35)

There will always be those groups of people who look down on others and who will mix and mingle only with the elite, the intelligent, the wealthy, and influential. I suppose associating with these types of people gives them a greater sense of self-worth and importance. "If I am with important people, I must be important, too." How unfortunate! Many of these associations are not deep friendships. They are more associations of advantage with a not-so-hidden agenda of what this person can do for me.

Seeking to be around influential people is not a bad thing in and of itself. There's an old Irish expression, "A dumb priest never got a parish." "Dumb," in this sense, means "not being able to speak." If we are going to change the world, we need to involve influential people. These talented people contribute greatly with their intellectual and even financial gifts, and they are able to make substantive change. The difficulty arises when our desires are limited only to those of a certain economic class or status of influence. As Pope Francis says so frequently, humanity cannot forget "those living on the peripheries." The needs of the disenfranchised must be in the heart of every Christian, and certainly in the heart of a priest.

There is an expression that I have heard many times since becoming a priest: "Chalices, not calluses." I would rephrase that expression quite differently: "Chalices *and* calluses." In other words, a priest's hands need to get dirty. My favorite expression of Pope Francis was spoken shortly after he became Pope in 2013. To the priests, he said, "Take on the smell of the sheep." In other words, become immersed in the world, be willing to get dirty, and spread the Gospel message beyond the four walls of our parish.

The days of people knocking on the rectory door are, for the most part, a thing of the past. When a priest ministers in the world, goes on to the "highways and byways," (Luke 14:23), "shaking the bushes," so to speak, looking for the lost sheep, it won't be long before the people of God (after finding the heart of God in the heart of a priest) desire to be near him, because being near him is like being near the heart of the Father. Every human person, the poorest of the poor, and the wealthiest of the wealthy, the virtuous, as well as the soul trapped in darkness, desires to sit at that table of the Lord, because it is from that table that all are fed and find love. The people of God, like the priest, share in this call and mission.

It has been said of people who work hard, "Don't overdo it! You'll burn out. Pace yourself." All of these statements can be true. The expression, "Hard work never killed a man" is false. Hard work can kill. Burning out is not healthy, and when it happens, a person loses ambition and desire and suffers greatly. As a result, those closest to this person are also affected by his or her pain. There can even come a point of not being able to function, and this helps no one.

With that being said, working hard is both noble and virtuous. "Emptying the tank," as I call it, is a sign of passion. By "emptying the tank," I mean giving of oneself to others, purely for the sake of Love Itself. St. Catherine of Siena once said, "Nothing great is ever achieved without much enduring." People who work hard change the world. They are full of desire. Their excitement for life is like a vibrant flame that burns in their heart. We are created by God for more, not less, and people who work hard strive to build—to create. They "empty the tank." For some, however, this motivation is solely for personal gain and personal profit. This mentality must change.

When a soul is converted from "I" to "thou," from "me" to "you," from self to God, that person desires to build in a different way—from the kingdom of "me" to the kingdom of God. As Scripture says, "Do not store up for yourselves treasure on earth, but treasure in heaven. For where your treasure is, there will your heart also be" (Matthew 6:19). We can't take our possessions with us. "Naked I came into the world, naked I shall return" (Job 1:21-22). No one has ever seen a U-Haul in a funeral procession.

In my twenty-five years of business, like any job (yours and mine), there are highs and lows—good days and bad—profit and loss. The very popular business expression, "the customer is always right," has much truth to it. All business owners aim to satisfy their customers to keep them happy. The old expression, "Everyone knows 250 people," is ever-present in the mind of a business owner. Good news can travel fast, but bad news travels even faster. Marc Antony's words from Shakespeare's *Julius Caesar* remind us that "The evil that men do lives on forever; the good is oft interred with their bones." (Act III, Scene ii) God forgives and forgets; customers often do not. "The customer is always right?" Yes, there is great truth to that. Good businesses try not only to meet a customer's expectations, but to exceed them. However, in every business, there are difficult (and sometimes even impossible) customers. At times, and in all objectivity, some customers are simply dead wrong. Hopefully, for most businesses, this is not the norm. In our case, we had very few customers that we would place in that category. Most customers have been a delight to work for.

People can be demanding. That's okay. Demanding people sharpen your skills and often raise the professionalism of a business to greater heights. Admittedly, it is most enjoyable to work for people who are easy-going, less demanding, and forgiving of little mistakes. These customers want to see a business do well and are happy to know that the business is making a reasonable profit. Some of these customers are customers for life, and friendships are formed. Some customers (few, thankfully) are the opposite of this, making workers feel like they are on pins and needles or under a magnifying glass, wanting to squeeze out every last penny. We worked very hard to try to please these customers, too.

Prayer in the workplace kept us together as a company. While it is certainly true that most major corporations succeed without prayer in the workplace, for our little company, it became our glue, our necessity, and a source of peace. In the current business climate, when people stay with companies for shorter and shorter periods of time, very often leaving for the next best offer, almost all of our employees have given us their entire working career. What they found with Sullivan Brothers was a low stress, peaceful environment, and a company that cared for them, their families, and the customers. We all want this in our lives and in our workplace. Work is a major part of our lives, and if the experience of work can be in a serene and peaceful environment, and the employee feels loved, needed, and respected, this is priceless.

So many people not only dislike their work but would even use the word "hate" to describe their job. They generally don't hate their work—what makes work impossible are the people with whom they work, whether it be a dictator boss, a company more concerned with the almighty dollar than with people, incompetence, laziness, self-interest, or in the worst case, all of the above. The secret to successful businesses essentially boils down to one word: love — love of customers, and love of employees. This may appear overly simplistic, but it is not. Obviously, this love (charity) has to be coupled with a good product and quality service. Without love, one's service is poor. Without love, desire and enthusiasm diminishes or even vanishes, thereby permeating every aspect of production. Love keeps a company together, and love keeps customers happy. In the same way that love builds up, sustains, and expands a church, so too love builds a business, a society, an economy.

Hard work is admirable; however, it needs to be said that rest is admirable too. In fact, rest is needed. We are not machines, powered up in the morning and shut down at night. The human person is not simply a functionary with a list of tasks each day to check off and complete. God created us with a necessity to sleep, but beyond sleep which rests the body, it is necessary also to rest the soul. Exercise, music, games, friends, and certainly prayer all rejuvenate our spirits and fill out our humanity. We become more completely what we are created to be when we include in our lives the proper balance of work and rest. "All work and no play" is an unhealthy place to be. All play and little work is even worse. As this chapter began, so it shall end, with a reminder from *Gaudium et spes* (24): "Man can only fully discover his true self in a sincere giving of himself." In other words:

Empty the Tank

"Take on the smell of the sheep," the Holy Father cried,
Spend your life for others — never seek to hide.
Tired? We will be.
Spent? It will occur.
Weak? We can expect it.
Yet, happiness is not deferred.
No one needs a priest? Few knocks at the rectory door?
Then where will we find the people? On the streets, in schools, and stores.
"Go and shake the bushes," the Holy Father once said,
And love until it hurts. We can rest when we're in bed.
Some seek a life of ease. "No heavy lifting," as some say.
What will be our legacy? We thought more about our pay?
Empty yourself for Christ— Philippians Chapter 2.
We will never be disappointed; rather, daily — remade new.
"Chalices, not calluses." How foolish a thought is that!
Chalices and calluses — real priests live for that.
Some fear they will be empty if they give it all away.
They know not what God does. He restores us every day.
As I end this little poem, if you'll allow me to be frank:
We'll be filled with Life, and Love, and Joy,
When we live to empty the tank.

—Fr. Jim Sullivan—

LIGHT AND HEAVY BURDENED   10

More will be said later about the privileged call to priesthood, but first I'd like to share a couple of humorous business stories, because the workplace is the common arena where the vast majority of people spend much of their time. Work needs to be serious, but work can also be enjoyable (at times even fun), especially when this time is spent with pleasant people.

Most business owners would be able to write a book about their many and varied work experiences, because business is essentially about people. People are beautiful and interesting. Their lives and experiences are rich fodder for stories, because business includes all types of people. In this sense, a workplace book could be a drama, a comedy, a tragedy… or a thriller! I'd like to spend a brief time on some humorous episodes in the workplace.

One Friday afternoon, my brother John, after finally completing a long, tiresome, and tedious job, wanted to beat the heavy weekend traffic home. As he was getting ready to leave, the customer asked if he could do a little favor by filling a small hole on a piece of wood siding. John had a can of "Great Stuff" in the truck, a material that is extremely sticky. It dries hard and can also serve as an insulation. As he took the lid off, the entire can spewed out uncontrollably, falling on the sidewalk, the porch floor, and his shoes; it made a huge mess. Needless to say, after now having to spend hours cleaning, he never made it home early. Sometimes the expression is true that "no good deed goes unpunished."

On another occasion, we worked for a very wealthy doctor and business owner. We built a beautiful two-story addition, matching the architecture of his home exactly. We were very proud of it. Two weeks later, I received a call, and on the other end of the phone was the wife of the doctor who exclaimed, "Jim, there's a hair in my stair!" I said, "Excuse me, Mrs. B.?" She said again, "There's a hair in my stair."

Wanting to please every customer but having no idea what she was referring to, I returned to the job. Somewhere on one of the stairs, an eyelash (presumably hers or her daughter's) must have floated and settled in the polyurethane of the new stair. At first, and in my presence, she could not see it or find it. About a week later, I received another call. With jubilation in her voice, "I found the hair! I found the hair!" It reminded me of the Scripture passage, "Rejoice with me, I have found my lost coin" (Luke 15:9). Unlike the verse in Scripture however, this scenario (most would agree) was a bit over the top. My brother returned to the job, and practically needing a magnifying glass, saw the very small piece of eyelash. He lightly sanded it and applied polyurethane. The customer was happy.

Sometimes in life we focus too much on the small stuff and are blind to the bigger picture. We expose every detail of a person's most minute faults and fail to see any good. We see, ever so clearly, the speck in our neighbor's eye but fail to see the plank in our own (Matthew 7:5). We cast a shadow over another's every thought, word, and deed, but excuse and forgive ourselves quite rapidly.

While it is true that the world includes many lost and darkened, even very sinful souls, the vast majority of people strive to be and to do good. Pope St. John XXIII once said, "See everything, criticize little, overlook much." In more common language, "Don't sweat the small stuff." Instead of magnifying the fault, a blessed virtue is to magnify the good. Strive to love a person as Christ does. This can be very difficult at times, but when we see with the eyes of Christ, the darkness of a person (and we all possess it in one way or another) is diminished, and we allow the person's light to shine through. If only we overlooked the faults and shortcomings of others in the same way we overlook our own. Lord, may I forgive others and love others the way You love me!

Allow me to share one more story. This may well be a story that has never before happened in the history of contracting! Early in our career, my brother and I were remodeling a bathroom together. As the homeowner was leaving her house in the morning, she informed us, ever so clearly, not to let her cat outside. "My cat is my pride and joy and has never been let outside. She (the cat) is not used to having people around, so you probably won't even see her. She will be hiding somewhere." My brother and I gutted the bathroom down to the framing, installed drywall on the upper half of the bathroom walls, and then went out to the truck for lunch. After lunch, we sheet rocked the lower half of the bathroom and began tiling the walls. At about 10 o'clock at night, we received a phone call from the distraught customer.

"Where's my cat?! My cat is not here!"

I said, "Ma'am, you said we probably would not see the cat, and we didn't. We worked all day, and barely opened the door."

"My cat is not here," she said in a panic. "I looked everywhere."

"I'm so sorry," I replied, "but we did not see your cat at all." Long story short, as she was brushing her teeth in the bathroom before going to bed, she heard a faint meow. It was coming from within the bathroom wall. While we were having lunch at our truck, the cat climbed in the wall and up through the framing, most likely out of fear. We came back to her home, tore down part of our brand new, beautiful tile job, placed some cat food in a dish, and her cat finally came out.

How can a story of a cat, running and hiding in the bathroom wall, possibly relate to the spiritual life of a human being? As human beings, we too can be afraid or lost at times. We often run to dark places to hide—sometimes for long periods of time. When in the dark (especially the darkness of sin), although we are not happy, and we know something is terribly wrong, we are often paralyzed. We feel unable to move or help ourselves. Eventually, (and hopefully, just like a cat's meow) we cry out for help, hoping someone will hear us. Some people are afraid of the dark. Some people are afraid of the light, because the light reveals too much and calls for a change in life, yet the enslaved person, truly paralyzed, prefers the darkness. "And this is the verdict, that the light came into the world, but people preferred darkness to light, because their works were evil" (John 3:19).

With sin and darkness, there is a very poor and temporary "comfort," but it never lasts long and always fills a person with a profound sense of emptiness. We ultimately desire to come out of the wall, the cave of darkness. The exposure to light, ultimately the Light of Christ, frees us. When we live in the Light and experience the peace that it brings, we later look back on our lives and will most likely cry out, "Lord, please give me the strength to never go back into that hole."

When we stand facing a bright light shining on us, where are the shadows that are caused by the light? The shadows are behind us. Every life has them. So too, when we stand before the Light of Christ, the first things we see when we get up in the morning are not the shadows or the phantoms of life (they are behind us); rather, we see the light. When we turn our back away from the light, namely the Light of Christ, where are the shadows then? The shadows are in front of us, and the further we walk away from God with the Light behind us, the shadows of life become even longer and larger. The proper stature of the Christian, in fact of every human person, is to face the Light. The darkness is then behind us, and we move forward.

Just like the cat seeking food, we too, with God's grace, move to the Light. We are hungry, but even in our hunger and thirst, we often move slowly. Fear and worry stifle us and prevent us from opening our hearts and our lives to both the light and food that nourish and sustain us.

"Come to me, all you who are weary and burdened, and I will give you rest. Take my yoke upon you and learn from me, for I am gentle and humble in heart, and you will find rest for your souls. For my yoke is easy and my burden is light" (Matthew 11:28-30).

Once we take the first step towards true intimacy with God, and feed on His delights, we desire more. Just as eating healthy food instead of continual junk food makes a person feel better in his or her body, so too does spiritual food. Ultimately, the Holy Eucharist nourishes the soul and propels us to greater delights found only in God. Like the cat climbing out of the wall, we again feel like we are safe and properly nourished and at home in the arms of Someone who cares for us.

Working in the building and restoration business has taught me many life lessons, the most obvious being understanding how nearly everyone in this world lives, works, pays bills, takes care of a house, and has responsibilities of a family. During the eight or more hours of work each day, we can experience the entire spectrum of both goodness and evil, virtue and sin. While life is going on, hopefully we simultaneously strive to keep God at the center of it all. While work has many joyful and even humorous stories to tell, every working person knows, all too well, that there are struggles and difficulties in the workplace. As one business associate once quipped concerning self-employment, "If it were easy, everyone would be doing it." Self-employed or not, work has its beautiful moments as well as its struggles. Hopefully, the joys outweigh the struggles.

Along with the many beautiful customers, there have also been periodic struggles. On one occasion, we worked for a man who was certainly of sufficient means. The job that we did for him came out perfectly, and the final cost was exactly as contracted. The man and his family went away on vacation, so the second and third payments were not made. Trusting him, we continued with the job, but when he returned to the beautifully finished basement, he simply did not pay the last ten thousand dollars. In this case, it was outright deception. There are people in the world who simply have little or no conscience. For you or me, we would not be able to sleep at night knowing we have deceived someone so seriously. Darkened souls are able to do so.

In a broken world, our consciences will be misguided if not well informed. The poorly informed conscience makes erroneous judgements, reasons badly and even sinfully. This customer violated one of the most basic principles of the natural law (what we know to be right or wrong simply by being a human being) by essentially taking (in this case withholding) that which belonged to another. We have all probably heard the expression, "Money is the root of all evil." This is actually a misquote from 1 Timothy 6:10 which says, "The *love* of money is the root of all *kinds* of evil." The verse continues, "Some people, eager for money, have wandered from the faith and pierced themselves with many sorrows" (1 Timothy 6:10).

Courts are filled daily with cases of deception resulting from one party or the other possessing a misplaced love for money or misguided sense of justice. When people in business suffer financial loss, it is a bitter pill to swallow and a difficult sin to forgive. May God have mercy on this man and all those who believe that deception of another human being is some sort of victory.

Another aspect of business profoundly related to spiritual life is loss. There is likely not a business in the world that has not suffered loss in one way or another. Loss can easily happen in the contracting business, because first of all, the profit margin is small. Secondly, the potential for error and unforeseeable circumstances is high. Inclement weather, untimely deliveries, human error, underbidding, not to mention the occasional difficult customer, all contribute to some jobs resulting in loss. These jobs are very painful, because the owners of companies actually take their own hard-earned money from savings to pay, at least in part, for someone else's new kitchen, addition, or the like.

Not all in life is gain. Anyone who has lived any reasonable length of days knows this all too well. Part of life is loss. The person who expects life to have nothing but the best of everything will soon be taught a hard lesson. While it is true that some people are blessed with good health, a good marriage, successful children, sufficient finances, and a long prosperous life, most people at one time or another encounter an unexpected cross. As previously stated, our crosses can bring us closer to Christ. For others, the cross may turn them away.

I recall many years ago hiring a new subcontractor who, it turned out, had a hidden drug problem. After giving him his next payment of $6,000, he took off and we never saw him again. The business was small at that time, and $6,000 was a lot of money for us. Instead of remaining angry and hurt, I asked God to bless six thousand people, one for each dollar lost. I prayed that our loss might be another's spiritual gain. I trust God answered this prayer and we will certainly know one day.

The losses we experience throughout life, when lived without a knowledge of the cross of Christ, can sometimes be crushing. As difficult and utterly painful as the losses of life can be, when configured to Christ and His suffering for us, we are given the grace to carry on one day at a time. For saints and those more advanced in the spiritual life, loss can even be turned into joy. God's grace does not necessarily make Christian living easy. God's grace makes Christian living *possible*. The crosses and losses of life are lighter when Christ is by our side, helping us to lift the burden.

TEARING DOWN IS EASY; LET'S BUILD

Perhaps the greatest lesson from the contracting profession is a lesson about destroying and rebuilding. It is very easy to destroy — to tear down. My brother and I once tore down an old building on a seminary campus that served as the chapel for over fifty years. The building was not small, yet it took less than one hour to tear down. The new chapel took eighteen months to build, sometimes with between sixty and eighty men on the job. Many of us sadly remember the tragedy of 9/11/2001. The Twin Towers of New York City collapsed in just under one hour and it took another thirteen years before the new Freedom Tower was completed.

The spiritual life, too, is easy to tear down. Sin is like the raging water of a flood; it cares little for what is in its way, and it leaves devastation and ruin in its wake. As Mother Teresa once said, "What you spend years building, someone can destroy overnight." Then she added the encouraging words, "Build anyway." Sin can do the same thing. It can sometimes destroy overnight.

Some sins eat away slowly and diminish us as human persons almost unrecognizably. People don't drink their first beer thinking they will one day struggle with alcohol. People do not begin to look at pornography thinking it will one day affect the way they view their own bodies, their very person, or the body of another. People are not born angry. The power of evil, the devil, truly is deceptive; we can be easily deceived, even causing us to think that there is little wrong in our behavior, while the entire time our spiritual lives are slowly eroding, and our love for God and others becomes colder. The devil is the great deceiver.

Virtuous acts, which at one time in our lives were habitual and performed with ease, can also slowly erode. Priests hear this all the time. "I used to pray all the time, went to church every week. Now, no more." Just like the sinful acts and addictions listed above, virtuous acts, when ceased to be regularly practiced, are slowly (and even sometimes quickly) forgotten. It is a common experience when a person begins to skip Mass just a few times; a new habit begins to form as old ones are forgotten. Before you know it, years can go by.

Christianity is definitely not for the faint of heart. Archbishop Sheen once said, "Dead bodies float downstream." It takes a living body to resist the currents of the world and to resist those things that entice us to forget about God. Just like a body needs regular exercise to stay fit, so too the soul needs regular spiritual "exercise" to remain spiritually healthy. Garbage in, garbage out! This is true for the body. It is also true for the soul. What we take in spiritually comes out in one way or another as virtue or vice.

Some sins are small and tear down slowly; other sins are big and tear down quickly. Drug addiction often leads to stealing, even from those we love. Drinking and driving can cause us to kill another person. Anger can lead to revenge in any number of ways, which seriously hurts another. Infidelity in marriage causes a rift and pain that is often too painful for a spouse to overcome. Deception at work may result in losing a good job, thereby affecting the entire family. The verbal or physical abuse of a parent or spouse can inflict lasting wounds. Indeed, sin does destroy and often destroys badly.

However, just as a building can begin to be built again after being torn down, so too, a person (after taking a good, hard, honest look at oneself) begins to realize, "This, or that, needs to go." We begin to build again, but this time, hopefully on a strong foundation.

Constructing a building takes longer —much longer — than destroying one. Yet in the spiritual life of a person, by God's grace and mercy, the opposite can happen. Years of sin sometimes end in a momentary decision and subsequently, immediate grace. The "rock bottom" (different for every person) is finally realized, and like a bolt of lightning, the person is awakened from living a life of self to a life of giving, from selfishness to selflessness, from "all about me" to all about others.

Sin wreaks havoc. Grace restores wholeness. This was the experience of St. Augustine. Years of sin and self-absorption were, by God's grace and the prayers of his mother, St. Monica, quickly brought to an end. One day while in a garden, he heard the voice of a child say, "Pick up and read. Pick up and read." He opened the Bible randomly to the letter of St. Paul to the Romans (13:13). "Put away the desires of the flesh and put on the Lord Jesus Christ." His conversion of 1600 years ago, through his life and writings, affected the entire Christian world for centuries. Sin, indeed, wreaks havoc; grace restores wholeness.

Many years ago, I recall driving to a home on a cul-de-sac to give an estimate for a proposed project. Every house on the street had been built within the last five years. It was an adorable neighborhood: beautiful front porches, well-landscaped yards, and an overall picturesque area. At the end of the street was one remaining foundation—the house had never been built. All the other houses had been attractively completed, and it was evident from the overgrowth on the property that it had been abandoned for quite some time. Not only as a builder, but as a person, I couldn't help but think to myself, "What happened? Was there a loss of a job? Perhaps a divorce? Maybe a financial crisis due to an illness? Perhaps a mistake in business that led to bankruptcy? Or maybe a combination of all those things?" Whatever happened, the foundation was laid, but the house was never built.

Building happens in the spiritual life too. Parents, very often, do the best they can in laying the foundation for their children. A foundation is the most important part, as well as the strongest part of any structure. A good foundation can be built upon, even many years later. It would be wise to spend sufficient time building your own foundation and that of your family. As best you can, make it strong, make it secure. Although at times there may be weeds and overgrowth, and it may appear that "no one's home" or God has abandoned us, know that the rock who is Christ gives us the ability, through faith, to build again — and to build beautifully.

IT FITS LIKE A GLOVE 12

During my many working years while owning and operating a business, from time to time some people would ask me, "Did you ever think of becoming a priest?" The answer was "Yes and no." Building and creating was my vocation; working with my body and hands, loving to sweat, coming home physically tired…this is who I was and am. It may sound a bit unusual, but I really did enjoy getting dirty and doing hard, physically demanding work. During those twenty-five years of business, I thought fondly about priesthood and deeply respected the calling, but I knew to the core of my being that priesthood was not meant for me. God was not calling. It was as simple as that. If the passion for the vocation to priesthood is not real, then a man should not enter.

Too many people live without passion. Passionless lives, lived day-to-day, never fully experience the fullness of what it means to be not only a child of God, but a human person. Passion is a necessary part of every vocation—of life itself. Very often, people find themselves stuck in jobs and careers for which they have little passion. While it is true that interests can change over time, and that people may desire to explore other career paths, sadly, due to lost pensions, benefits, seniority, and advanced age, people find themselves at a point in their careers where it is nearly impossible to leave their jobs and change to something for which they've discovered a passion. Many simply cannot financially afford to do so, and they are stuck. Changing careers would mean economic suicide for the family. When this happens, and a career change is nearly impossible, hopefully other passions in life develop more fully—hobbies, interests, friendships, family, and of course, faith. While it is true that our work is a significant part of our daily lives, when we view our work (no matter how menial or difficult our job is) as helping to build the kingdom of God, our work cannot only become tolerable, but peaceful. This is especially true when one resigns oneself to the fact that God is the Author of one's work and one is living for a greater good.

Priesthood came to my mind from time to time. It was never ruled out, but as I said, the desire was not there. I vividly recall one bitterly cold winter day. We were installing a roof on a new house. Twelve inches of snow had to be shoveled off first, the wind chill was extremely low, and the conditions were just miserable. While bundled up, and working on the highest ridge of the house, I raised my hands in the air and called out to God with all my heart, thanking Him for my vocation as a contractor. Almost no human person on earth would want to be in that frigid place at that moment, but God gave me the grace to be thankful to be where He called me at that time of life.

During these years, I was still very involved in the Church, teaching religious education to teenagers, assisting at parish events, and from time to time, praying Eucharistic Adoration. The sudden death of my older brother, Bill, on St. Patrick's Day 2003 had a powerful effect on me. Death affects people differently. We have many funerals at the Basilica—approximately 125 each year. There is no cookie-cutter way to grieve; it is different for every person. Some people are changed forever by the death of a loved one. Whether that person dies old or young, for many people the loss can be a lasting trauma. The sadness may be lessened slightly over time, but the interior loss is still present. For others, there can actually be happiness and gratitude in the heart of a person when a loved one passes. This is generally for a person who died older and after a full life. If both the deceased and the ones left living behind are people of great faith, this makes the loss less painful and tragic. Some people may even say, "I'm happy for her. She's met the Lord whom she loved."

The very day my brother Bill died, after the initial shock and later in the evening, I felt an inner peace. Without getting into every detail of his life, I was confident that it was his time, and trusted that he was with Christ. A few months after his death in the spring of 2003, I saw an announcement in the parish bulletin indicating an upcoming class for new deacons. Someone had previously said to me, "Did you ever think of becoming a deacon?" I immediately answered, "No. Priest or nothing, and I'm not called to be a priest." Summer faded into fall, and the announcement was no longer in the bulletin, but the date stuck in my head: a Sunday afternoon in October. What I'm about to share is both amazing as well as somewhat humorous.

After Sunday Mass, I came to my house; it was 1:00 p.m. The advertised deacon program popped into my mind, and I thought to myself, "Is it today? Why not? I'll call and see what it's about." I called the diaconate office, and to my surprise (because the offices would have been closed on Sundays), a woman answered the phone (she later told me that she just happened to step back into the office to get pencils that she had forgotten). Stumbling over my unprepared words, I blurted out, "Uh, hello, is that *deacon thing* today?"

She replied, "Excuse me…'deacon thing'?"

I said, "Oh, um, I'm sorry. I mean the deacon class."

She probably thought to herself, "Oh, here's a real winner!" She said, "Yes, it's today. It starts in one hour. Everyone has been signed up for months."

"Oh, sorry," I said. "I saw it in the bulletin a few months ago and just thought I would call."

After asking a few questions and with some hesitation, she said, "Well, I guess you can come." One o'clock. A one-hour drive. I made it to the seminary at exactly 2 o'clock. If that is not the hand of God, I don't know what is. Long story short, and after a five-year program, "giving it a shot" turned into a beautiful calling and I was ordained a deacon in 2008.

Still running and operating a very busy business (we generally had over fifty jobs going on at one time), while at the same time serving the Church in ordained ministry, was for me, a dream come true. Having an active life in both the world and in the Church brought great joy. It fit me like a glove, and in that same glove was the hand of God. One Sunday while serving as a deacon, during the Consecration, as the priest lifted the Host, the thought of priesthood again came to mind, and immediately I said to myself, "No. It doesn't get any better than this: deacon and business owner." I was living my vocation.

During my time as a deacon serving four churches in the working-class town of Torrington, Conn., from time to time parishioners (mostly elderly women) would say, "You should be a priest." I would, of course, respond, "Thank you," because no matter which way you look at it, it's a beautiful compliment. These statements became more frequent. One Saturday afternoon, after the Vigil Mass, an astute, likable, yet rugged retired police officer said the same thing, but this time in a way others hadn't. He looked me in the eye, firmly shook my hand, and said the exact same words: "You should become a priest." Yet this time, for whatever reason (God's time, I suppose), I began to think more about it, and priesthood began to take on an added appeal and desire.

God has a calling for each of us, and we will be happiest when our response is in conformity with God's call. What is typical for young people today (and of course in times past as well) is when we reach a certain age, we begin to sift through our many likes and dislikes to choose a career, and we then choose the one that appears to be the most appealing. I encourage young people not to simply make "lists" of the many good options the world offers, but to do much more: namely, to ask God what He wants for your life. The vast majority of people do not ask the Lord, Who knows us best, what His plan is for us. Rather, we make these all-important life decisions (and others like it) solely on our own, or perhaps with the help and advice of a loved one. The Lord Jesus loves us, and He desires to guide us in the important decisions of life.

To find God's will in our lives, both praying and then *listening* are required. For those who pray, we are generally very accomplished at the asking part. But very few know what it is to truly listen. My father used to say, "We have two ears and one mouth. Let's use them in that proportion." In other words, listen twice as much as we speak. Very often, we speak twice as much as we listen.

Being a good listener is also very beneficial in our human relations. No one can bear to be in the presence of a "talking-machine" for long—the person who does nothing but talk—talk—talk and never listens. Communication is a two-way street. Imagine a friendship with one person doing nothing but talking, and in particular, asking. That friendship would get old very fast.

In our relationship with God, many people do little more than ask—ask—ask, and that asking generally comes only in a time of need. "Ask and you shall receive" and "Give us this day our daily bread" are beautiful forms of prayer, and God certainly desires us to reach out in our need, but prayer is also much more than simply asking. The best human relationships have both receiving and giving, talking and listening. The same holds true in our relationship with God. Periods of praying are to be reciprocated by periods of listening, and in that time of listening, we will find the answer to the deepest questions of life that we all seek.

Can God speak in noise? God can do anything. God can speak in noise. The more important question is, "*Does* God speak in noise?" God rarely speaks in noise. God speaks in silence, and if we are to truly find the answers to life's deepest questions (and in particular, those that have to do with our future), significant time needs to be spent in silent listening. This is, indeed, one of the great secrets of the spiritual life; in a world full of noise and distraction, we often find ourselves uncomfortable in silence and can't wait for it to be over. St. John Vianney, the patron saint of parish priests, once wrote of the Christian sentiment that desires to spend little time in prayer, "I will only say a couple of things to you (God) and then I will be rid of you." We will flounder through life spiritually if silent prayer does not become the very fabric of who we are.

The Lord desires us to choose the proper vocation for ourselves, the path where we can best serve and ultimately become holy. When we do, we become the best spouse, the best single person, or the best priest or religious. When we choose poorly and make those all—important decisions without Him, God fortunately does not abandon us. The Gospel, after all, says some people "bear fruit thirty and sixty and a hundredfold" (Mark 4:20). God, in fact, complements all three. In every major decision in life, young and old alike: *pray and then listen.* When you choose the vocation for which you were created, you will bear an abundant harvest, and just as importantly, you will be happy.

One wonderful woman in whose home we worked back in the contracting days and long before my priesthood, told me later that she sensed in me that I should be a priest. She began to pray for that. How can one ever express enough gratitude for such kindness? May I encourage everyone reading this to pray for your priests, and to pray for future vocations? There is not a crisis of vocations; there is, rather, in the world today, a crisis of faith. Young men and women are out there, and they are willing to give of themselves sacrificially, for the good of the Church and the world. They need to be inspired — filled with God's grace. When this happens (*when*, not *if*), young men and women will be standing in line, desiring to serve and share the greatest message of all: Jesus is Lord, loves us, forgives our sins, and desires us to live with Him forever. On behalf of my brother priests, I say thank you to all who are praying for us.

Allow me to deviate further for another moment and speak more specifically about vocations to the priesthood. A beautiful evening occurred at the Basilica. I believe our parish Son, Blessed Michael McGivney, was very much behind it. At our monthly deanery meeting (a gathering of priests from the same general area), twenty-two of our parish pastors discussed, among other items of business, vocations to the priesthood. We decided to ask each parish in our local deanery to invite one man to come to an evening of discernment. It wasn't an evening specifically for priesthood; rather, it covered married and single life, too. Essentially, it was for young men asking for God's will in their lives.

Would ten men come? Fifteen? At the Basilica at all Sunday Masses, we prayed for forty men, the biblical number of testing (forty days of fasting, forty days on Mt. Sinai, forty days of rain in the days of Noah). Long story short, seventy-two men came, with another ten who wanted to come but could not. It gave us priests a deeper realization that our young men and women are beginning to realize more and more that they both need and desire more than what the world offers. The next evening, thirty-three women came to a Women's Evening of Discernment.

Discernment Nights, Basilica's McGivney Hall (2023)

These seventy-two men and thirty-three women felt strength together: a feeling that they were not alone, that there were others their age who saw the world differently and not through the typical secular and materialistic lens. Of these seventy-two, won't you pray with me that twelve become priests? And of the remaining young men and women, that they become the best of fathers, mothers, and single people? The second step never happens before the first, and unless we encourage and pray for priestly vocations from our own families, how can we expect great things to happen in the Church? When we move with God's grace, all things are possible.

I have a humorous story to share. Prior to making the decision to enter seminary (and, yes, I, too, was asking and also listening), I decided to get away from the business and spend some quiet time on a pilgrimage in the Holy Land. I wanted to be near the very place where Jesus lived and walked, suffered, died, and rose.

One night while in Jerusalem, I took a walk to the church built on the site believed to be where Mary was born. I was the only one in the church and felt the presence of God there. With the flickering of a multitude of candles casting reverent shadows, there was an interior peace in this little place. After praying for a while, I left and walked the nearby street filled with shopkeepers. Most of them, due to the late hour, had closed; however there was one shop still open, but ready to close for the night. I was admiring a beautiful chasuble (a priest's outer garment for Mass) that was hanging near the store entrance. I had no intention of buying it; it was simply very attractive, with a red Jerusalem cross on the front and back.

The shopkeeper saw me and immediately said, "Do you want it?"

I said, "No, I'm just admiring it; it's very nice."

"One hundred thirty-five dollars," he said.

In my mind, I thought it would be $500. "No," I said, "I'm not a priest. I would have no need for it." "

One hundred fifteen dollars," he said, with an unwillingness to let me go.

"Thank you, sir," I said. "That seems very reasonable, but I simply don't need it."

Little did I know, and found out later from our tour guide, that it is a practice, perhaps with a little superstition, that the Jewish shopkeepers in the Holy Land desire to close a sale with both their first customer of the day and their last.

I began to slither away, and he called out, "$95!"

I, too, called out and said, "Sir, I'm a deacon. That is a priest's vestment. Thank you, but I have no need!"

It Fits Like A Glove

Thanking him and now starting to walk away a little more briskly (and admittedly getting a little disturbed at his persistence), he gave one last ditch effort and yelled out, "$75!"

For $75, I thought, "I'll give it as a gift to a priest." So I bought it.

Yes, God is full of humor and surprise. That chance encounter provided me with a chasuble from the holiest land on earth, even before entering seminary.

Epiphany Sunday, Church of the Assumption, Ansonia, Conn. (2019)

The Holy Land trip brought peace to my decision to enter seminary. In the same way that men and women "know" when they have found their spouses, so too, I knew that the Lord was calling me to leave what I loved and to follow Him to greater love and service.

The most difficult part of the decision was telling my brother and leaving the business. I love my brother John dearly, and there are few business partnerships in the world like ours. We had complete trust in each other. Neither one of us ever "measured" or "kept score" of the other's time spent on the job or in the office. We have joked that in terms of time spent on jobs, one of us probably owes the other a great deal of money, but we don't know who it is nor do we care. By God's grace, we also agreed on every major business decision. It really was, and still is, a beautiful relationship.

So many people have warned, "Don't go into business with family." It is true that many good friendships and family relationships are destroyed in business partnerships. Sometimes the struggles are over money or future vision, and a big one has to do with time. "You're not pulling your share. I'm doing more work than you." Fortunately, John and I never had any of these struggles. I miss the business, and I am happy to say that they are doing very well without me. God has continued to bless them.

When I told John that I believe the Lord was calling me to priesthood, he immediately said, "I knew this day would one day come." It happens so often that people closest to us see things that we don't see within ourselves. How often it also happens, in dating relationships, for example, that someone may later say, "I knew from the start that he or she was not the one for you to marry." For good or bad, we can learn from our mistakes. Still, our life choices must be our own. Another can guide, encourage, and make suggestions. However, for people to be at peace with themselves, the final decision must be theirs.

With my brother and business partner John on my last day at Sullivan Brothers, Wolcott, Conn. (2012)

There have been children who have essentially been forced into professions that they didn't freely choose. "There's going to be a doctor in the family." It happens in the priesthood too, admittedly more in years past. Some have termed it a "mother's vocation." These priests are never truly happy because the choice was never their own. There are doctors, teachers, businesspeople, and priests who often wander, never experiencing passion, because someone else chose their vocation. They did not want to disappoint Mom and Dad or the family name and wanted them all to be proud. The repercussions of someone else's choice for our lives eventually surface in the form of sadness and disappointment and sometimes even other destructive behaviors. Freedom is a wonderful gift from God, and it is a tragedy when it is taken from us. Family pride and "what will people think?" can blind parents, and children can end up with passionless careers and even passionless lives.

People often emphasize what the priesthood is not, or what it doesn't have —wife, children, grandchildren, companionship, money—the list goes on and on. Because a person cannot picture a happy life for oneself as a priest or religious sister or brother, one assumes it must be difficult and unhappy for everyone. Yet, vocation surveys show that the priesthood possesses among the highest "job satisfaction ratings" of all. My own priesthood is certainly in this category. Once the realization of God's call was made clear, I knew that I would love being a priest. I can now say after just over ten years, I did not know I would love it this much. The world view of priesthood is a big NO!: no to a family, no to making money, no to personal freedom. In my view, priesthood is rather a resounding YES!: yes to giving God everything: my self-will, body, time, desire, service. Whatever our calling (but in a unique way in the priesthood), do not be afraid to give Christ your "yes" — your all. You will not be disappointed.

While it is true that priests don't have our own children, we have countless spiritual children. Many children, and in a special way, those from broken or fatherless families, look to the priest as a stable male figure in their lives. Are priests lonely? I'm sure some are. Many married people are lonely, too. There is a big difference between being alone and being lonely. The happy priest is alone, but not lonely. Every human person suffers in some way from that innate loneliness that is the result of the fall of Adam. St. Augustine tells us, "We are made for God and our hearts are restless until they find rest in Thee." As the song goes, sometimes we are *"looking for love in all the wrong places"* (Mallette, Morrison, and Ryan). God alone satisfies the inner loneliness that every human heart experiences. We will never be completely whole until we are joined to Love Itself.

The life of a priest is a joy-filled life. I will qualify that by adding, *if* one is called. The life of a priest, like any other vocation in life, can be difficult, and for some, even miserable. Marriage is a beautiful calling, but it can also entail great suffering if one is not called, or if one or both of the spouses makes it difficult, even unbearable. Some people don't believe the single life is a legitimate calling, and instead believe that it is a life not of choice, but of default. Having lived the single life for decades before becoming a priest, I completely disagree with this manner of thinking. The single life can be one of profound self-sacrificing gifts, and as a result of this gift of self, the person is also filled. The extended family of a single person can be large and, consequently, the life of the single person can be one of great happiness.

One of the greatest mistakes of our society today is that people do not ask God for what path they have been created. This trend has been happening for decades, with the result often being poor choices in jobs, careers, and spouses. It is simply assumed that a man or woman in their twenties or thirties should marry, and if they are not married by a certain time, "there must be something wrong with them." There's an old expression, "Marry in haste, suffer at leisure." As I stated earlier, marriage is a covenant (a sacred bond), not simply a contract between two people. In an imperfect and fallen world, mistakes and poor choices are made by the most thoughtful and intelligent people. Bringing God into the choices of career, spouse, and vocation elevates the possibility that our choice is the best one for us. God does not want to see us miserable; rather, God wants us to be happy.

While it is true that the Lord can bring good out of bad, we serve best and live best when we choose properly. We live less, desire less, and struggle more when we choose poorly. I believe we would find that if the majority of people were asked the question, "Was God a part of your important life decisions?" most would say "No." God has a will, a plan, and a purpose for all of us. Finding it is like finding a great treasure; and that treasure, rather than losing luster and brilliance over time, instead glows because the heart is happy. I knew I would love being a priest. I had no idea I would love it this much.

LIFE TO THE FULLEST, CUM PASSIO

13

In the book of Revelation, God speaks of passion: "So, because you are lukewarm, neither hot nor cold, I will spit you out of my mouth" (Revelation 3:16). While passion is admirable, not all passion is virtuous. A person can be passionate about the wrong things: excessive power, possessions, pleasures, popularity. These four "P's," while not bad or sinful in and of themselves, can consume a person when not sought in moderation. Pursued to excess, these passions ultimately become a passion for living solely for self. Taken to the extreme, they lead to emptiness in life – a dead end – because although they drive people (sometimes throughout their entire working career and the whole of life itself), they never fully satisfy. The glow and excitement that once motivated us each day diminishes at the end of life and can even result in sadness and depression. We begin to realize that we lived for the wrong things.

Socrates once said, "An unexamined life is not worth living." All people, at one time or another, very often in sickness or old age, have to look back and honestly ask themselves, "What did I live for? What was my most important and greatest passion in my life?" Everyone has an answer to that question.

I have often expressed in homilies the following: "Show me how you spend your time, and I'll show you what you love the most." What is it in our lives that we love the most? It could be any number of things: a hobby, family, exercise, career, God. We spend as much time as we can with those things in life that bring us enjoyment, contentment, and passion. We avoid those things that do not. A daughter of an ailing parent once said to me, "I spend all my days, even years, caring for my parents. This is not the way I had planned to spend my middle-aged years." I encouraged her and said, "This is time you will never regret."

The deepest expression of love is self-sacrifice, and the deepest lovers are those who are able to give of themselves for the sake of the beloved. Like Christ, we, too, are called to live *cum passio* (with passion). This is what He did for us. "He emptied Himself, taking the form of a slave" (Philippians 2:7). He did so to atone for our sins and show us the way to eternal life. Sometimes our time is spent doing things we should not be doing (sin), sometimes things we truly enjoy doing (gift), and sometimes things we prefer not to be doing but do anyway (grace). Time is a gift. It is to be used wisely for our own sanctification and for building up the kingdom of God.

There is a mystery in human suffering that we often do not fully realize in this life. We may have to wait until the next life to discover why things happened the way they did. "Show me how you spend your time, and I'll show you what you love the most." How we spend our time shows exactly who we are as persons. Hopefully, for every person reading this little book, if it has not already occurred in your life, it soon will: that you spend quality time on elevating your spirituality and seek to fall more in love with the One who loved you into existence.

One of my dearest childhood friends describes himself as a devout atheist who happens to be married to a very devout, practicing Catholic. He is one of the kindest, most generous people I know. Although a man of no religious faith, he is passionate about life. He is a very successful scientist and simply does not see the possibility of God as a loving creator. For him, the cosmos exists, and human beings evolved over time from lower life forms, and here we are. He believes we possess an afterlife; however, that afterlife consists in us living on in the lives of others. In other words, our good works and actions make the world a better place, and we live on into the future by our good actions and influences. He may never come to Christ through the "head" or the intellect by the teachings of the Church. As I wrote earlier, goodness and beauty can also bring a person to faith. My friend may come to Christ, even become passionate for Christ, by being touched to his very core through one experience or another of the beautiful.

As he (and for that matter, countless others) approaches retirement age, I have a feeling what is going to happen at some point before his death, is that a breakthrough of grace will occur. Older age often brings a person to think about death in general, and his/her own personal end in particular. This is the great hope for anyone reading this book who has a family member or loved one who seems to be miles away from any form of conversion to a life of faith. Where doctrine, dogma, teaching, and catechesis fail to inspire, beauty and goodness almost always do.

The greatest passion in the world is, of course, a passion for God. Passion for God far exceeds any of the passions solely for this world. Faith elevates, raises up even the most mundane of activities, because faith gives life. Golf, cooking, studying, music, reading, work—all of these things are elevated because with faith, we perform our tasks and enjoy our hobbies knowing they are gifts from God. When we advance deeper in our faith, we begin to view every aspect of our life, the good and even the suffering, with a greater awareness of the One who has granted the gift (or allowed the cross) for our wellbeing. Faith removes the scales from our eyes and allows us to see the deepest meaning of life more clearly. Christ, alone, mends our brokenness and restores our passion for living and he does so *cum passio*.

"FRIEND, MOVE UP HIGHER" (LUKE 14:10) 14

In 1978, after being elected Pope, someone said to Pope John Paul II, "This must be the greatest day of your life, being made Pope." He said, "No, the greatest day of my life was the day of my Baptism." We may recall from our grade school catechism that in the Sacrament of Baptism we are "born again with water and the spirit" (John 3:5). Original sin of Adam is washed away, we become children of God, and the gates of Heaven are opened to us. We receive an indelible mark, a character, and are configured to Christ. Baptism is, indeed, the greatest day in our lives! When a baby is baptized, part of the sacramental celebration is to place a white garment on the infant. This garment represents purity and being clothed in Christ. The very words being spoken by the priest or deacon are, *"You have become a new creation and have clothed yourself in Christ. May this white garment be a sign to you of your Christian dignity. With your family and friends to help you by word and example, bring it unstained into eternal life."*

We are all sinners. Somewhere around the age of two, we are already beginning to learn and then speak the word "no" and to express our own self-will. Every human being has to humbly admit, in one way or another, whether it be in a big way or small, that we are sinners. We have all said "no" to God when we should have said "yes," and we have said "yes" to sin when we should have said "no." Sin offends God, often another person, and always ourselves, because sin diminishes us as human persons. The Church, the family of God, is also diminished, because we are all connected, we are all part of the same family. To say that my sin (even a private sin that no one else sees), has no effect on another is like saying my pollution affects only the place where I throw my garbage. The family of God is diminished when one of its members is lessened by sin. In the same way, the Church, and humanity itself, rises to a higher and greater place when even one person is baptized and (please God) goes on to live a virtuous, holy, and pure life. "I tell you, in just the same way there will be more joy in heaven over one sinner who repents than over ninety-nine righteous people who have no need of repentance" (Luke 15:7). Every human person has, in one way or another, tarnished their baptismal garment by sin. Yet that soiled cloth, by God's amazing grace, can be made white and pure again.

My favorite verse in the entire Bible is Luke 14:10. It is a story of a man who, at a feast, sits in the lowest place. The host then invites him to a greater place with three words: "Move up higher" (Luke 14:10). This is the continual call of Christ to all of us, to come from wherever we are in our own spiritual lives to a higher and greater place, a place of deeper love and intimacy with God. As I mentioned earlier, the human body weakens over time; however, the heart is not meant to follow suit. An old body with a "weak" heart, namely a person who in his or her older years still lacks love, is a person who has sadly missed life's higher calling and has remained spiritually in a very low place.

It seems to me that the papacy of Pope Francis is characteristic by two primary Christian visions: the first being mercy, and the second being joy. If we are to "move up higher," we need to both experience mercy and joy and give (live) mercy and joy to others. In our weakened and sinful nature, in our proclivity towards sin and selfishness, mercy heals and joy restores. The Bible says, "All have sinned and fallen short of the glory of God" (Romans 3:23), "Even the just man sins seven times daily" (Proverbs 24:16), and "The one who says he has not sinned is a liar, and the truth is not in him" (1 John 8-10). When Christ's mercy and joy are both discovered and then lived, the deepest virtues of Christian life continue to be more deeply sought. We have experienced the best of God and cannot help but desire to share that best with others.

In describing new life and living in the Light of Christ, Mother Teresa used the image of a painting. From a distance, the artwork may appear to be perfect, and if there are any imperfections, only the artist will know. When a light shines closely on the painting, however, the imperfections are more readily revealed. So too, when we live in the Light of Christ, the true Artist of every human person, we see our faults and imperfections more clearly. This revelation is not to be feared; rather, it can be embraced, because it is in the discovery of our faults and weaknesses that we can begin to grow anew. Psalm 19 says, "Lord, cleanse me from my hidden faults." Once they are revealed to us, we are to treat ourselves with mercy and experience transforming joy.

An additional word about *joy*. St. Teresa of Avila once said, "From sour-faced saints, good Lord, deliver us." The true Christian life is one of joy, not a somber spirit. Many of the great saints, St. Philip Neri being one of them, were known not only for their joyful hearts, but for their humor and playfulness. Christ says in the Gospel of John, "These things I have spoken to you so that my joy may be in you, and that your joy may be full" (John 15:11). Archbishop Fulton Sheen was once asked the question that has been asked from the dawn of mankind: "What is the meaning and purpose of life?" He replied, "The meaning and purpose of life is to be supremely happy." Life in Christ is never simply average or mediocre. Comfort is mediocre happiness, because comfort never fully satisfies. Comfort is not joy. Comfort deceives us into thinking it's all that there is, that the world has nothing more to offer. True joy is found only when lived in communion with the source of all joy—Christ Himself.

Sometimes even very devout people are seriously lacking in manifesting joy, to the point that they rarely, if ever, smile. This can be a dangerous spirituality and will attract no one to the Christian faith. A person who, for whatever reason, believes that Christian living is only and always somber and serious, is severely in need of this most basic Christian tenet. Some believe that the beautiful practice of reverence is somehow contradictory to joy. Joy and reverence, however, are not opposites. They go hand in hand, and the true Christian lives both. Since Christ is fully human (along with being fully Divine), then Christ, too, would have been joyful. While on earth, it would have been a joy to be in His presence (He would have laughed), and it is a joy to be in His presence now.

UNLESS YOU BECOME LIKE A CHILD   15

At the core of the human person is the innate desire to be pure. Even the person who does not know or follow God admires purity. Why? Because we are wired to be clean, not dirty. In the Gospel of Matthew, the leper cried out to Christ, "Lord if you will it, you can make me clean." Jesus responded, "I do will it. Be made clean." (Matthew 8:2) We know, in our deepest instincts, that the body —the human person— both desires and deserves to be treated purely. We are a temple of the Holy Spirit where God dwells, and we are created in His image and likeness (Genesis 1:26). If conversion of the world back to the Light of Christ is going to happen, society's attitude toward the human body, marriage, family, human sexuality, and ultimately to the dignity of the person must drastically change.

When it comes to the Ten Commandments, essentially nine of them pose little opposition, even for those who practice little or no faith. Only the distorted conscience, for example, would propose theft (per the seventh commandment) as a noble act. No person supports jealousy or envy (the ninth and tenth commandments) as admirable. Few would promote idol worship, false gods, or foul language (the first two commandments) as something beneficial. Although many are blind to the sin of abortion, few would encourage outright murder (the fifth commandment). As weak human beings, we often commit these and other sins, and when we do so, because of the way God made us, most people will experience a disturbance in the soul, a sullen interior feeling. Sin is not a joyful experience; it is a sad and disturbing one.

The one commandment most disagreed with is the sixth

commandment, "Thou shalt not commit adultery." At the age of fifteen, while at Sunday Mass, the priest in his homily gave a brief synopsis of the Ten Commandments. When he came to the sixth commandment, he held up his large right hand, and simply said, "When it comes to the sixth commandment, remember these five words: No sex outside of marriage." This means that married couples are to remain faithful to each other, and that single people are not giving themselves away to someone to whom they are not married. This manner of thinking is so far removed from the lived experience of our society, that even some devout people reading these sentences may be thinking, "Father Sullivan, what prehistoric rock did you just crawl out from under?" Others may say, "Get with the times."

    I would, instead, suggest that "the times" need to get back to God. If, in our current hookup and pornographic society, the world was also witnessing strong families and packed churches, one may convincingly point to the positive fruits that flow from such behaviors. This would be strong evidence of a society moving in the right direction, becoming more virtuous. This, however, is far from the reality of our current culture. The behaviors of recent decades have slowly, but surely, eroded the basic moral fiber of our society and have led to the current depraved spiritual climate. The expression, "the proof is in the pudding" is imminently true. In more Biblical language, "By their fruits, you shall know them" (Matthew 7:20).

    There are many factors that have led to the crisis of marriage, family, priestly and religious vocations, and church attendance. One brief answer would certainly include our nation's increased wealth as compared to past times. Material comfort is almost always accompanied by decreased devotion. While obviously not inherently bad, comfort deceives us into thinking that we are self-sufficient, that we don't really need God. When we are "filled," one of the first things that "goes" is our level of and desire for religious faith.

Technology, too, has advanced our society in so many ways — communication, computers, cell phones, economics, entertainment, medicine, the list goes on. Closely linked to these advances, however, is a serious distraction from the deeper realities of life—relationships with family, friends, private prayer, and spending time with God. We have been distracted from the very meaning and purpose of life itself, and slowly lulled to sleepiness, leaving little room for God.

The causes of our current struggles with marriage and family are extensive and cannot be fully covered here. That being said, a third reason often overlooked is the use of contraception and the world's contraceptive mentality. Perhaps you are again thinking about that prehistoric rock from under which I crawled? Allow me to explain further. Without getting into the history of contraceptive use (it's a very interesting study), let's begin by simply saying that prior to the 1930's, every Christian denomination condemned it as sinful. Currently, the only mainstream denomination to stand clearly against contraceptive use is the Catholic Church. Pope Paul VI, in his 1968 Encyclical "Of Human Life" (*Humanae Vitae*), essentially said there exists in human intimacy an unbreakable link between life and love. Like all principal bodily functions (eating, sleeping, drinking), intimacy's first purpose is also to be life-giving. Secondarily, attached to intimacy is pleasure, just as it is to rest and nourishment. When our pleasure is the primary objective of any of these bodily acts, there is a separation — what Pope Paul VI called a disorder. The act of intimacy is prevented from completing its intended, God-given outcome.

The whole purpose of contraception (and by that is meant every form of contraception: condoms, pills, diaphragms, implants, spermicide, tubal ligations, vasectomies) is either to kill the sperm or maim the egg, namely to prevent the sexual act from being life-giving. What follows may be difficult to read, but in reality, with contraceptive use, every act of intimacy contains within it a certain death to the possibility of life.

The human person is composed of both body and spirit; that is how God made us. We are not simply a body; we have a body and a soul. Because of this intimate relationship between body and soul, what we do with our body affects our soul, our spirit — our very person. When every contraceptive act of intimacy is opposed to life, to say that this has absolutely no effect on the soul is simply naïve. Plainly stated, contraception affects the soul and affects love, because there is an objectification and inherent selfishness attached to it. Since the sexual act is prohibited from giving physical and biological life, at some level, it also affects and diminishes love, itself, between the couple.

Pope John Paul II writes in his "Theology of the Body" that human intimacy is, at its core, a form of prayer—a way of giving praise, thanks, and worship to God. There is not a church on the face of the earth that is saying this in the same way as the Catholic Church. How often have we heard, when it comes to human intimacy, that the Catholic Church is a big "No?" But it's actually just the opposite. The Church elevates intimacy to a place that no other church does, proclaiming that intimacy is, rather, a huge "Yes," at the right time (in marriage), and with the proper person (one's spouse). Any act different from this is, in fact, on some level, an act against purity itself, and it makes marital intimacy less than what it is created to be.

What has been some of the fallout from our now decades-long use of contraception? While it is certainly true that there are many causes for marital and family struggle, it is most interesting to note that for those who do not use contraceptives in their marriage, the divorce rate is somewhere around 3%. In society as a whole, the rate of divorce is approximately 50%. If a couple, along with not using contraceptives, is also generous with their time, talent, and treasure and practices their faith, the divorce rate is essentially nonexistent. These statistics are taken primarily from Dr. Janet Smith's study *"Contraception: Why Not?"*

Engaged Couples' Conference Mass at the Basilica (2019)

One of the joys of my priesthood is marriage preparation. Along with celebrating many weddings, the Archdiocese also offers Engaged Couples' Conferences to prepare couples for their future life together. More and more in recent years and even decades, couples are already living together prior to marriage. Yet, whenever we give a conference on the *Theology of the Body,* including contraception, they all say almost universally that they have never heard this Church teaching before. Many couples see this teaching as inherently beautiful, and I believe they are beginning to be awakened to a new way of viewing the body and human intimacy. This teaching is eminently countercultural, but it is also eminently attractive. We are created to be pure in all things, and when we are, the floodgates of the soul are opened. God's grace and Divine life are allowed to enter with a resulting leap in happiness and peace of soul. Simply stated: we are wired to be pure.

Purity of one's body is not promoted in our current society. Media, commercials, TV, and internet have all, instead, encouraged a hook-up culture, easy sex, and "friends-with-benefits." Many people, young and old alike, but especially the young who are at the age of self-discovery, know inherently (especially when they are casually intimate) that what they have done with their body is disordered. There is then a disturbance and pain in the soul, because we know that we have fundamentally given ourselves away at the wrong time, or perhaps we have been used by another. Many young people (and even older people many years later) seek counsel and healing from past (even buried) pains. They are confused about how they feel, because our culture preaches that nearly every form of deviant behavior or lifestyle is permissible. Guilt and sadness should not be felt, and if they are, they can be attributed to an antiquated view of the body or from some form of oppressive religiosity.

In our innate desire to be pure, we will seek to find purity somewhere. Instead of striving for bodily purity, we rather seek a misplaced purity, perhaps to ease the conscience from our rampant, disordered impurity. The new "clean" is more concerned with earthly cleanliness at the expense of moral cleanliness: recycling, energy efficiency, green technology, composting, and carbon footprint concerns are a few examples. These are all very good initiatives, in and of themselves. Pope Benedict XVI and Pope Francis both strongly promoted care of the environment as a moral obligation, because the world in which we live is a gift from God and is to be cared for. In 2010, in his message for the Celebration of the World Day of Peace, Pope Benedict said, "We are all responsible for the protection and care of the environment." Pope Francis, in his encyclical, *Laudato Si,* speaks extensively of humanity's responsibility to care for the world that God has graciously gifted to humanity. The call from God is not a case of *either/or* (purity of body or purity of environment), but it is rather a case of *both/and* (purity of body **and** purity of the world). The cleanliness of the planet has, in many ways, replaced the moral "cleanliness" of the human person.

Changing society's attitude and belief system concerning bodily purity in both courting relationships and marriage will be like reversing a tsunami. Until we see the human body as a temple of the Holy Spirit in which God dwells, we will continue to experience a drowning of the soul. If human dignity is not discovered through a life of faith, society may begin to shift its manner of thinking (and behavior) to one of greater purity by simply witnessing the fallout that has occurred from our deviant living and the sadness that always follows in its wake. Marriage and family life (and children, in particular) have suffered greatly. We are created to live a certain way, but when we follow our own path and not that of the Creator, the soul cries out for healing. This "crying" of all of society may be the initial spark for a pure heart. May it then ignite into a flame of authentic love!

Although, perhaps, getting a bit off track for a moment, an antidote to the use of contraception needs to be briefly presented. Otherwise, couples who may have legitimate reasons to delay pregnancy (economic, psychological, family needs, etc.) and want to be faithful to the Church will find themselves with no other reasonable choice. Couples often believe that, immediately after their honeymoon night, a pregnancy will result. While this is certainly possible, many couples (approximately 1 in 6) who are open to life struggle to achieve pregnancy. Others are surprised when, after stopping the use of contraceptives, pregnancy does not always occur when they expect. Without getting into great detail, for those who, for just reasons, need to limit their family size, Natural Family Planning (NFP) is an all-natural, Church-approved means. NFP is not Catholic contraception, because it works in conjunction with a woman's natural, God-given cycle and those times when the woman is most likely to conceive. NFP, when used properly, is over 99% effective — more effective than any artificial contraceptive, while at the same time respecting the relationship between life and love. Couples who use NFP begin to find that, although difficult at times, they learn to love each other in more non-sexual ways. Their marriage can actually be enhanced greatly, because both body and soul, life and love, are more deeply cherished. For more information on NFP go to: https://www.usccb.org/topics/natural-family-planning/.

If you haven't yet thrown the book away, or in frustration closed it due to the preceding paragraphs, I end this chapter by expressing with all my heart the need for purity in all things. Sins of the flesh are not the worst sins in the world. Sins of pride are. Pride, in a certain sense, puts us in competition with God and also our neighbor. Sins of the flesh, although not the worst, make us *feel* the worst, because they are sins against our own body — our very person. St. Paul says, in his First Letter to the Corinthians, "Every sin that a man commits is outside his body; but the fornicator sins against his own body" (1 Corinthians 6:18).

Innocence is a beautiful virtue. God, at His core, is utter simplicity. The Bible instructs us to be "as wise as serpents, but as innocent as doves" (Matthew 10:16). This innocence does not, in any way, mean childishness; rather, we are to be pure and child*like*. "Unless you become like a child, you shall not inherit the kingdom of heaven" (Matthew 18:3). Innocence and purity bring happiness, not sadness. The world is often blind to this. The human heart ultimately desires to be pure: pure of heart, pure in speech (what we say), pure in our eyes (what we desire to look at), pure in our ears (what we desire to hear), pure in our attitude and disposition, and pure in our body. True innocence is not naiveté. Humanity, at the very core of our being, desires it. Innocence is a gift from God, and when lived and practiced, it manifests the deepest inner beauty of a person and reflects who God is.

Many years ago, while at a small conference of teenage Confirmation students, a number of guest speakers spoke of their beautiful, yet sometimes tumultuous, conversion to Christ. From drugs, alcohol, sexual indiscretion, anger, and selfish rebellion, it appeared as if the speakers were attempting to outdo each other in terms of their level of deviant lifestyle, each implying that their own conversion was more dramatic than the next — that God "saved me more." The students were given the impression (not purposefully) that to be close to Jesus, one must first fall, and even fall badly.

I raised my hand, somewhat squeamishly and with hesitation. Not trying to be judgmental in any way, I shared with the teenagers that one does not have to go "down" before coming "up." In other words, a young person does not have to experience the worst of sin before experiencing the best of Christ. While it is beautiful to have a tremendous conversion to Christ after a "life of dissipation" (Luke 15:13) like the Prodigal Son and then become a saint like Augustine or Mary Magdalene, it is also beautiful to become a saint like the innocent St. Maria Goretti or St. Aloysius Gonzaga. Both these saints were young, yet they knew in their hearts that the heart of Christ is pure, and that we are happiest when we, too, seek that pure heart and strive to embody it.

From our earliest years and continuing to grow throughout our lives, Christ can be loved, and faith can be practiced. A return to the purity in our youth (indeed for people of all ages) will give us the joy that we all ultimately seek. The innocence and purity of God radiates from the soul that possesses it. It is not "cool" to be bad; rather, it is edifying and desirable for a young person to live a life of sanctity and to be good. How often it happens that this profound truth is not realized until our later years. Thank you, Lord, for your unfailing Mercy!

Most priests, I'm quite sure, would agree that among the greatest pains people express to them are pains involving the body, either committed against an innocent, unwilling person, or committed against themselves. Purity, as previously mentioned, involves every aspect of human life — mind, body, thoughts, attitude, desires, and dispositions. If the world (or for that matter, any individual person), is going to be converted to Christ, then the axis of our hearts that has tilted away from Christ for so long needs to return to Purity Itself. True conversion will never happen without it. We end as we began: "Lord, if you will it, you can make me clean." And Jesus responded, "I do will it; be made clean" (Matthew 8:2).

STRONG AND GENTLE 16

A few brief words regarding both men and fathers need to be penned. Having been in the working world for the majority of my life, and particularly the contracting profession, I have a pretty good idea of where most men are in their spiritual lives. This may appear to be a blanket statement, but overall, men desire to be seen as strong and to feel strong about themselves. In no way do I mean to convey the popular Hollywood, macho, completely independent, "tough guy" image. Some men, perhaps many men, desire to be portrayed this way, but many do not.

Universally, however, every man wants to feel strong in his character — in his person. He wants to feel that he is strong in his resolve to be able to say "No" when he should say "No," and to be able to say "Yes" when he should say "Yes" — to be strong in the face of opposition or even injustice. No man wants to be viewed as weak or as a wimp. It's simply not in our DNA.

Stated most basically, if the world is going to be converted to Christ, men have to change. Men excel in so many ways. We are good workers, providers, coaches, and life teachers. However, when it comes to the spiritual life, all too often, men are weak and dare I say, wimpy. Men are generally not opposed to religion or to a life of faith; it's simply "not for me." There are men who believe that loving God and living a life of faith is for those who may need a little life crutch — for those unable to make it on their own — for those more dependent and needy. Worldly strength, although beneficial in certain ways, can also be a cover-up, a façade for what is spiritually lacking inside.

Many years ago, when I was in my early twenties, a nun gave me a banner that read, "Nothing is so strong as gentleness. Nothing is so gentle as real strength." Gentleness is not a sign of weakness, as many men believe; rather, gentleness is a signpost for an interior strength, because the gentle and humble soul rises above our weakest human instincts that often want to react harshly, and sometimes even brutally. From whence does this true interior strength come? How is it acquired? Every man wants it, but few realize that it comes from a relationship with Christ. Yes — to follow Christ is *manly*.

Christ, alone, brings a man to the fullness of his manhood: what it truly means to be a man. When a man is strong and in love with God, he is also stronger in every other aspect of his life. We become better husbands, boyfriends, workers, and citizens. We are all weak in one way or another, but just as the person who never exercises the body will never be strong in the body, so too, the man who never exercises his spiritual life will never be fully awakened to the fullness of his manhood. He may be the greatest athlete, have the strongest body, be the smartest, the wealthiest, the best CEO, but his spiritual life will be desolate. A man without a spiritual life attempts to fill it with other things — none of which fully satisfy.

In the life of a priest, it is somewhat sad (and at the same time strangely humorous), to walk into a room where many men are gathered and be the "elephant in the room." A good example might be at a stag, sporting event, or public activity that involves only men. More often than not, these activities include those who are not practicing a life of faith in any way. When a priest wearing his clerics walks in, you can almost hear the silent screams, "THERE'S A PRIEST IN THE HOUSE!" Men at all costs avoid his gaze, because they fear that the priest, who acts in the person of Christ, may be able to see into his very soul, and he is ashamed of what may be seen — that his weakest places will be revealed. Like the gaze of Christ to Peter after his denial, the exposed soul may need to "go outside and weep bitterly" (Luke 22:62).

In the days of Christ, the leper was avoided like the plague. No one wanted to be near him out of fear of being infected. The priest is, in a certain sense, a modern-day leper, not because he is contagious with a disease, but because his very presence challenges, even pricks the conscience of the distant soul. This is a good thing, because the priest may remind him of his isolation and separation from God and perhaps even his sin. If a man is rarely reminded of goodness and holiness, he is quite comfortable remaining in his darkness. The darkened soul prefers to hide rather than be challenged or exposed in any way. When alone on his pillow at night, however, he may think, even if briefly, of his life and his need to change — his need for God. If troubled in his spirit, he hopes to fall asleep quickly or remain in some varied form of hurtful distraction. If you want to see big, burly men become weak as puppies, observe them as a priest enters a room, and all too often, they will scurry like fearful kittens.

Just as many men avoid being near a priest, many priests fear being near ungodly men. The experience is too foreign and uncomfortable for them, because they are more accustomed to being near men in church settings. As a result, both priest and men avoid each other. This is a great sadness, because many men who strive to appear strong and "together" are actually weak and looking for another man to talk to without shame. These men often have very gentle hearts and are ripe for conversion. The pull and pressure "to be like all the other guys" or to live up to some sort of false masculine image prevents many from revealing their innermost longings and pains.

I thoroughly enjoy being with this type of man and in this type of setting, because I see so much possibility and potential. It was also the setting in which I worked in the contracting profession for so many years, and I have come to deeply love these men. The desires of multitudes of men are misplaced, and they need someone to show them the path to true manhood — what it truly means to be a man of God. Who better than a priest to do this?

It is said that Waterbury's Fr. Michael McGivney had an infectious personality. He also understood the heart of men and the importance of their roles as fathers and husbands in the life of the family. As a priest, he experienced firsthand the amazing capacity in a man for virtue and goodness while also recognizing his capacity for weakness and failure. From alcoholism, to indifference, to abandonment of the family, he saw men both at their worst and at their best; he understood their need for God.

On a December evening in 1881, a young man by the name of James "Chip" Smith shot and killed the police chief of Ansonia,

Connecticut while drunk. He was eventually executed. Fr. McGivney's regular priestly presence at the New Haven prison converted Chip Smith's hardened heart. His heart slowly tilted toward a love of God and a peaceful acceptance of his impending death without fear. Fr. McGivney was able to "see" into the heart of this troubled man in his great need.

There are many Chip Smiths in the world…At the core of their being, all men desire to be known, understood, and ultimately forgiven and loved. A man (in particular, a priest) who lives in communion with the Source of all Love is blessed to be able to give men what the world rarely offers.

In keeping with this idea, and on a bit of a light-hearted note, a number of years ago on a summer evening as my sister, Sr. Veronica, was driving through a remote section of Connecticut, her car broke down. The sisters live very simple lives and generally do not travel with a cell phone. The car just happened to break down outside a biker bar. My sister had no choice but to enter and ask for the use of a phone or for assistance. The bar was crowded with many rugged-looking men. Needless to say, there was very likely a lot of drinking also going on. When my sister walked in the bar, nearly the entire place fell silent. I would bet my bottom dollar that this was the first time a nun had ever walked into this bar wearing a full religious habit. All these men probably thought the second coming of Christ was upon us!

Once my sister explained her situation, these big, burly men who also have big burly hearts, were practically crawling over each other to see who could be the first to help the nun in need. My sister was back on the road within 15 or 20 minutes.

Situations like that of my sister remind us of the power of faith to soften all hearts – even the hearts of men who are in their own spiritual "biker bar." Men need to again realize that faith is not only for women and children. Deep faith is manly. Faith is not a sign of weakness, but of profound strength. Until men begin to realize that their spiritual lives, or lack thereof, affect entire families, the family—and all of society—will suffer. I call all men to unite — to get that part of our lives in order — so that we can witness the beautiful things that God will do through us. How the world will change!

On the road to Emmaus, two men are traveling and encounter Christ on the way. We can all ask ourselves the question, "Whom am I walking with in life? Who is at my side? Who do I desire to be there?" Who we desire to be with says a lot about who we are as men. Perhaps a man wants no one at his side. He is a maverick, a lone ranger sitting high upon an isolated horse, sure to show little emotion and little need. Men need not be ashamed to say that they desire Christ to be their companion. In fact, we can glow with pride. Real men love. Real men "need," and the best men are those who walk the walk of life with Christ at their side.

God bless our women and our mothers. In the Bible, although twelve men were chosen to be apostles, it is the women in the Bible who consistently seek Christ. Mary Magdalene, the woman at the well, and the hemorrhaging woman are just a few examples. In the present day, it is women who are more involved in the vast majority of parish activities.

Statistics, however, show that when a father is faithful and lives a life of faith, so do his children; this happens approximately seventy-five percent of the time. When only the mother practices her faith, the children do so less than twenty percent of the time (https://promisekeepers.org/). This is not, in any way, to say that if a child grows up in a faith-filled household and then decides not to practice his or her faith, that it is necessarily the parents' fault. Many parents suffer from this experience, blaming themselves for their child's loss of faith or their indifference. Children grow up with so many societal influences and are often pressured to make choices that are not always of God. Children, even from the most devout families, wander and sometimes wander badly. Keep praying for them and have Divine hope for their return. Keep in mind that we, too, may have done the same when we were their age.

A brief word about peer pressure. Peer pressure can be a terrible negative force away from spiritual growth. We may think of peer pressure as something which besets only the young, but it is actually an affliction of every age group. I fondly remember an amicable ninety-plus year-old Dominican friar who once said to me when I was in my early twenties: "Jimmy, you know one good thing about being my age?" "No, what's that, Father?" I asked. He paused, ready and anxious to give the punchline, then added, "No peer pressure!" We both laughed, because almost all of his peers were dead. There is actually much wisdom in this, because there are pressures to conform at every age. These pressures can be a tremendous obstacle to conversion, because the pressures to conform are generally very secular and worldly, and very often not of God, the sacred, and those things divinely ordained.

Our society has been drawn relentlessly to this "enlightened" method of thinking, and if one dares to stand against it, the labels of *intolerant, bigoted,* and *narrow-minded* begin to fly. Certain companies have fired employees, because their thinking is no longer in line with the more progressive vision of the company. Christians, and Catholics in particular, because we hold to traditional values especially on matters of marriage and family, are often labeled as antiquated and even "dangerous" to society. These pressures are real for all ages, and if people are not already strong in their faith, and their Christian consciences are not properly formed, they can very easily begin to find themselves slipping into conformity with the whole of society under the guise of tolerance and even mercy.

Young people are particularly susceptible. What young person desires to be seen as odd or different from everyone else? Young people already have a hard enough time growing into their own bodies, finding their way, and loving themselves without also being attacked or ostracized for holding onto traditionally held beliefs. Let's face it—it's easier to bend, to conform, and to give in than it is to remain firm, consistent with belief, and resilient in faith.

The desire to conform and to even be seen as not particularly religious begins at a very early age. Along with being a pastor, I have also been an administrator of two Catholic grade schools. Our children begin and end their school day and each snack or meal with prayer. Even the youngest children in Pre-K, aged 3 or 4, innocently, and with great devotion, hold their hands together in prayer unabashedly and even proudly. Kindergarten children point prayerful hands to Heaven as little angels. First graders know God exists, and with heads bowed and hands raised, they show that they truly believe it. The same beauty and innocence hold true for second graders. Without fail, somewhere around spring of third grade, the prayerful hands once raised in childlike faith begin to come down, and self-conscious awareness of what others may think begins to set in. All of us know, all too well, that it does not stop there, and as we grow up, we may prefer to be thought of as "with the times" and just like everyone else. We will give our greatest opinions on sports, workplace issues and recipes but will remain in utter silence at the water cooler when people speak against God and the things of God. Worth repeating again are the words my brother heard the Lord say to him on his own life changing day of denial: "Whoever is ashamed of me and of my words, the Son of Man will be ashamed of when he comes in his glory and in the glory of the Father" (Luke 9:26).

All this being said and having deviated for a moment to discuss children, if a parent is weak or indifferent in his or her faith, the child will almost always be too. Very often when adults come to a life of faith in their later years (this happens frequently), they feel regret over the fact that they may not have been the best example to their children in this regard, and that things could have been different in the lives of their children if they, themselves, had known Christ in their earlier years. While it is certainly true that some fault can be placed on parents, whether purposeful or through ignorance, I remind these parents and all who are reading this book that faith is a gift, and it comes at different times in the life of a person. Had you known Christ previously, things would have definitely been different in your own life and perhaps, too, in the lives of your children. Because of Christ's amazing mercy, from this point forward, you may shine like the stars and the Good Lord may do more with your later-in-life faith than if you possessed it from the beginning. As scripture says, "Those who lead the many to justice shall be like the stars forever" (Daniel 12:3).

For those who are younger parents, may I humbly urge that if Christ is not already a part of your life, ask for the great gift of faith, and then do the best you can to live it to the fullest. A preacher was once asked the question, "How do I get my children excited about their faith?" The response: "Get excited about yours." This is, of course, not a guarantee, but it certainly gives the best chance. All children, although they may indicate otherwise, want to know God, because they ultimately seek to know the Source of everything. They want to see God in their parents, and in a particular way, in their fathers. The axis of humanity that tends to tilt away from God will again turn toward the Light, and families and societies will blossom "when fathers again turn to the Heavenly Father" (Malachi 4:6).

THE RAIN IS GONE — 17

Sometimes, we find ourselves filled with hops. You may be thinking, surely you mean "hope," not "hops," don't you? Actually, I mean both. The 'e' in "hope" will come in Chapter 19. Hops, of course, is one of the principal ingredients in beer; attempting to be clever in the title, I simply mean those "ingredients" in our lives that attempt to fill us and distract us from what is ultimately most necessary and satisfying to God.

St. Thomas Aquinas once wrote of the value of "moderation in all things." He didn't mean, of course, moderation in charity (or other virtues), rather in those practices taken to extremes that can pull us away from God. There is nothing wrong, of course, with enjoying a glass of beer or wine; however, excess can cause great problems for both families and for the person. Our culture sees all too much of this. The addictions of life can be a disaster for our bodies, our families, and our souls.

As a priest (and for that matter, a former contractor and business owner), I have witnessed them all: drugs, alcohol, gambling, lewd, inappropriate sex, overeating, pornography, gossip, and the list goes on. Addictions are not limited to any particular race or class of people. Doctors, teachers, athletes, the working class, teens, men, and women of all ages and social classes can be affected by any of the various forms of addiction.

Severe addicts are consumed in their daily thoughts (sometimes continually) by the next hit, the next bottle, the next sports bet ("it'll be a winner"), sex partner, or opportunity to eat. Anyone who has struggled with addiction knows all too well the standard routine: the temptation comes, then the voices begin to speak. "You deserve it," "You've worked hard today," "It will be good for you," "You're not really hurting anyone," "This one will be the last," "You're stressed and it will relax you." After a battle of either little or great length, or sometimes with no fight at all, we find ourselves once again indulging.

The temptation sometimes comes gradually; not so, however, the aftermath of self-loathing and self-accusation. These always come quickly. We instantly feel deceived again. Shortly after the failure, we again have a new resolve, maybe even new strength and readiness, to go into battle to fight again. Then, after a period of time, the length of which depends upon the severity of the addiction, we are again faced with the convincing voices of deception, and the vicious cycle begins again: we fall, we get up, and then the sadness, strength, failure, new resolve, and self-disappointment begin again. For the vast majority of addicts, there comes a point, very often after years of living this vicious cycle, when a person begins to realize, "If I'm going to conquer this, if I am going to rise from this darkened abyss, I'm not going to be able to do it alone."

The day of turning back towards a ray of light is often referred to as "hitting rock bottom." When that rock bottom day comes after years of both self-convincing and self-deception, it can be the beginning of a glorious time in the life of an addict. Many addicts remember clearly (and may even celebrate in some way) the day new life was found. After many years of drinking, one of my dear friends caused a drunken head-on collision. Fortunately, no one was seriously hurt. That was his final rock bottom. Since that day, which included a deeper realization of the reality of God in his life, he says everything got better. "The sky looks bluer, colors are brighter, my food tastes better, and even my relationship with my wife is more beautiful." When the "hops" are gone, whatever they may be, a new horizon is revealed and new possibilities discovered.

I'm reminded of the 1972 song by Johnny Nash, which contained the lyrics, "I can see clearly now, the rain is gone. I can see all obstacles in my way." Worldly clarity is a wonderful start, but Christian clarity is so much more, because with Christ in our lives, we begin to see the root causes of those things that kept us away from conversion — from fully living. Then as the song continues, we can sing from the rooftops, *"It is going to be a bright, bright, bright, bright sun-shiny day!"*

Sadly, for some, "rock bottom" is death. For others, it comes after losing a house, getting caught in adultery, seriously injuring a person, losing a job, serious illness after wild living, or even after accidentally (or purposely) killing someone. We begin to realize that our own self-absorbed life has tilted well beyond 23 1/2 degrees away from God and has nearly flat-lined. The resuscitative breath of God calls us back in mercy and gives us another chance, another opportunity, for new life to begin again.

Yes, for many, the *hops* of life have caused us to tilt away, well beyond the 23 1/2 degrees. How about the rest of us? 20°? 15°? 10°? 5°? Need we be concerned? Is my life "not that bad?" How often do we think, "At least I'm not where he/she is?" Like the Pharisee in Scripture, "Thank God I'm not like the rest of men: liars, hypocrites, reprobates" (Luke 18:11). Just as the addict can be self-deceived, so too is the self-proclaimed "angel." This type of deception can actually be worse, because a person sees no need to change anything.

We have all heard the expression, especially somewhat popular in recent years, "outside the box." It means, of course, to think more creatively and approach things (business, life, work, problems) from a different perspective and view situations from a different angle. The same routine and doing things the "way we have always done them" can, at a certain level, continue to survive and even thrive, but "same old, same old" in the spiritual life not only gets old, it leads to spiritual stagnancy and even death.

For faithful people who have known God since their earliest years, there needs to be a certain caution. The practice of religion can become so habitual (weekly Mass, Holy Days of Obligation, fasting and abstinence on designated days), that spiritual growth is sometimes unrecognizably slow. These faithful and good people may become so accustomed to the standard weekly routine, that growth in faith or thinking that there can even possibly be more in one's spiritual life, is far off their spiritual "radar screen." These are generally the same good people mentioned in Chapter 8 who love God the same at eighty years old, as they did at sixty, as they did at twenty-five years old, as they did as teenagers. They are living in spiritual parentheses, so to speak, and never come to realize that there is more beyond the enclosure. Not only don't they seek more, but they may not even be aware that more can potentially exist.

This manner of thinking describes a huge population of Christians. At the lowest level, the "nice guy" mentality (one who may or may not have a strong belief in God) may even think himself a living saint. This becomes not only a blindness to sin, but an ignorance that sin even exists. This complacency is a terrible plague to the spiritual life of our society and is one of the principal reasons why faith (and therefore life itself) becomes mediocre at best and completely stale at worst. Prior to every funeral, I ask in the gentlest way about the deceased person's spiritual life. How often a priest will hear with enthusiasm, "He went to Catholic High School and was an altar boy!" But that was sixty years ago.

The realization that there is more of God to know and love can happen to anyone at any age. I recall many years ago, when I was in my late 20's, standing in the confession line in the Basilica where I am now Pastor. A man that I had known through some parish associations was in front of me, and when he came out of the confessional, he said to me in tears, "After all these years, I have finally come to see the light." He was always a practicing Catholic, but something must have happened that day in that confessional (or in the days leading up to it), that brought him to the next level in his spiritual life. There can be blindness at any age. Sin does that. But just as there is always another layer of an onion to remove to get to the core, so too in the spiritual life, there is to be a continual stripping away to get to the core which is Christ.

Shortly after my brother John and I started our business, we began to hire employees. One of our younger employees was wonderful: on time for work every day, loved by the customers, and a hard worker. An employer could not ask for more in terms of presentation and appearance. The problem was that he was simply not catching on with how to be a good carpenter. His skills were not developing. For a moment, we were actually thinking of letting him go. Then one day, just like the 75-year-old man in the confession line, he "got it" and eventually became a highly skilled craftsman. The same can happen in the spiritual life. What seemed to be locked in parentheses all of a sudden opens, grace enters, and a new life begins. The old mentality of "punching in" to Mass and "checking the spiritual box" is over, and a new horizon becomes visible.

This change can, at first, feel like a sad day, because we may now, for the first time, reflect on time wasted, talents lost, and years spent living for the wrong things. During this "lost" time, we may also realize that we scandalized people, committed sin, and offended a loving God. Archbishop Sheen once said, "Sin is not the worst thing in the world." We may be thinking, "What?! Sin is not the worst thing in the world? What could be worse than that?" Sin deceives, sin separates, sin weakens, even destroys. It affects our relationship with Almighty God and everyone around us. What can possibly be worse than that? He then goes on to say, "The denial of sin is worse." People who realize they are sinners at least remain in a circle of truth. We know and are aware of our need to turn, that there is room for improvement, for greater virtue and deeper love. We pray weekly at Mass, "*I confess to almighty God and to you, my brothers and sisters, that I have greatly sinned, in my thoughts and in my words, in what I have done and in what I have failed to do, through my fault, through my fault, through my most grievous fault; therefore I ask blessed Mary ever-Virgin, all the Angels and Saints, and you, my brothers and sisters, to pray for me to the Lord our God.*" There is great humility and freedom in knowing that we are sinners. Christ can easily work with the humble. But the self-righteous, self-proclaimed "angel" is a tougher nut to crack. Indeed, our hops can tilt into hope.

HURTFUL. HEAVY. HOLY. 18

We know from Sacred Scripture that every human being will, at one time or another in life, like Christ our Savior, have a cross to carry. It seems like a paradox when Christ, on the one hand, says, "Take up your cross and follow Me" (Matthew 16:24), while at the same time saying that "My yoke is easy and my burden light" (Matthew 11: 28-30). We may well ask, "Well, which one is it?" because "burden" and "easy" don't normally go together; in fact, they are rather contradictory. "Burden" and "cross" are equated with pain and suffering, while "easy" denotes comfort. The best of ease and happiness are to be found in the next life, and the journey for everyone in this life will include (along with joys) different levels of pain and suffering. Although it does not always seem to be the case, we are told in Paul's First Letter to the Corinthians that we "will not be tested beyond our ability" (1 Corinthians 10:13).

In life, there are essentially three variations of the cross. These crosses, depending upon their weight and severity, are among the reasons why some people depart from a life of faith or never pursue it in the first place. If God is a God of mercy and compassion who loves me, then why are these bad things (whatever they are) happening to me? We may expect life to give us mostly ease and little suffering. The cross, understood in the context of a loving God, is a concept very difficult and sometimes almost impossible to understand. For others, the cross, as difficult as it may be to carry, becomes a means of grace, spiritual growth, and holiness of life. Some people depart, while others are drawn closer to God through the cross.

The first cross is perhaps the most difficult; it is the cross that we bring upon ourselves. It can include sinful decisions that affect us, sometimes permanently. Sins of anger, revenge, theft, impurity, infidelity, careless driving, abuse, and abortion will all have painful and potentially lasting results. These sins sometimes happen quickly and impetuously, but more often than not, they are the result of an interior disturbance that has taken root over time.

No one is happy in sin, because sin brings deep sadness, regret, and even self-loathing. A darkened conscience and soul begins to feel in the midst of its sin, a distance from both God and people; feelings of being worthless, unforgivable, and unlovable can then follow. Sometimes people even blame God for their actions. "How could you have allowed me to do what I did? Why did you not save me? Reveal yourself to me? Show me that I was on the wrong path and about to make a very serious mistake?"

The five steps to conversion (intellect, preaching, beauty, tragedy, passage of time) have already been discussed, but hopefully the person with the "self-imposed cross" will discover one of them and begin to realize that God's grace truly is amazing and can heal the most burdened life and heart. We can again feel redeemed, lovable, and forgiven (by God and ourselves). When we do, the weight of the cross begins to be lifted, and self-imposed guilt is slowly removed; life is again worth living.

The second cross is very different from the first. The second cross is caused by another person, sometimes willingly and purposefully and sometimes accidentally or by reason of neglect, foolishness, or ignorance. Drunken driving has caused the death or injury of many. Financial corruption by a CEO can place a family or business in desperate need. Inner office underhanded politics gave someone else your well-deserved promotion. Someone falls asleep at the wheel and you are the one to receive lasting injury. A spouse has a better attorney, lies in court, and you lose the kids. Maybe you have been cheated out of your fair share of an inheritance.

These crosses are immensely heavy too. These crosses do not require self-forgiveness, but rather picking up the pieces, doing the best we can to live with what happened, and moving on as best we can with our lives. Forgiveness of the person who hurt us is a process, but unless it happens, we can potentially remain in continuous anger and resentment. Perhaps what pains us the most is when people who offended us, who caused our pain, are indifferent to what they have done to us or even rejoice in it.

People who are able to move on with life and even come to accept what another person has caused are deeply virtuous people. There is an old expression, "The person who cannot forgive digs two graves: one for himself and one for the person not forgiven." An unforgiving spirit can tear us apart and eat away at us. It wounds *us* more than the person who hurt us. Forgiveness is as much for oneself as it is for another. The wounded heart seeks the freedom that only forgiveness can give.

People are often very confused as to what forgiveness entails and what it does not. First and foremost, forgiveness does not mean that we have to like the person who offended us. Nor does it mean that we have to try and repair a relationship as if the hurt never happened. Particularly in close familial relationships, we do our best to continue with some semblance of a relationship, but sometimes that, too, is perhaps not possible. Depending upon the offense, the person who offended us may even be detrimental to be around. One's presence is too hurtful, perhaps even dangerous. What forgiveness *does* mean is that we are not going to allow the offense to dictate the remainder of our lives and that we will strive to live as closely to Christ as we possibly can. Christ is the source of love and mercy (for our sins and the sins of others), and if we are going to live in peace, we need to live connected to the Source of peace.

When one expresses to me in spiritual counseling that he or she is consumed with anger and hurt, I ask, "Are you able to pray for the person who hurt you?" The answer is generally a mixed "yes" and "no." If yes, that is a great place to be, because it means we do not desire the demise of the person who offended us. We desire their conversion, and it does happen, at times, that two people who were once separated due to hurts of varying degrees, are again reconciled.

If the answer is no (I can't bring myself to pray), the reason often given is that the hurt and anger are so deep, they are unable to even *think* of the person. Doing so causes pain and anxiety too great to endure. In that case, I encourage fervent prayer for the *desire* to one day be able to pray for the offender. As was mentioned previously, if we do not give our pain to Christ, we will (in one way or another) give it to another, or it will be bottled up inside and come out in other hurtful, painful, and unhealthy ways.

In praying for someone who hurt us (or in at least seeking the desire to do so), I regularly remind the hurting people that the one who offended them would likely not have done so had the offender been in a deeper relationship with Christ. Sin, and the hurtful things that flow from sin, would be far less likely had the offending person known Jesus more intimately. We pray as best we can that the people who offend us come to a deeper realization of who Christ is in their life. We are blinded by sin and act accordingly when immersed in it. We see clearly and act accordingly when Christ is the delight of our eyes.

For some, the third cross is the heaviest; for others, it is the easiest to bear. This third cross is not the result of our own sin or foolishness, nor is it caused by others — whether purposefully or accidentally. The third cross is one allowed by God. Some may say or believe it is *caused* by God, because God, being all knowing and loving, could have (or *should* have) prevented whatever it is that is now our cross. "God is in no way, directly or indirectly, the cause of moral evil" (Catechism of the Catholic Church, 1993, para. 311).

    Sin and death entered the world with the Fall of Adam and Eve. In a weak and fallen world, bad things happen — yes, even to good people — even to innocent people. God is still All-Knowing, All-Powerful, and All-Loving. It takes time and great faith to come to accept our unexpected crosses and, generally, even more time to understand them. Very often the understanding part does not happen in this world, and we may never know why things happened the way they did until one day when we meet our Savior. In the life of a priest, we see, all too often, sudden and unexpected accidents, illnesses and cancers, and even tragic deaths. These are among the most difficult instances of bringing comfort to people, because the cross is so unexplainable — so incomprehensible.

    I recall a number of years after the war in Afghanistan, listening to a soldier saying that losing his leg was the best thing that ever happened to him. What? The *best* thing that ever happened? Yes! By God's grace, he came through his loss to understand the deeper meaning and purpose of life. He said he would have never arrived at this place of peace without the tragedy. Another man who had AIDS (Acquired Immunodeficiency Syndrome) said, "I'd rather have AIDS and know Jesus Christ than not have AIDS and not know Jesus Christ." At our deepest level, we have to try as best we can to trust that God is still with us, loves us, and that somehow, we will be okay; God knows all things.

    It is true that certain events in life are so painful and so tragic, that we may wonder how anyone can live through them. There is a permanent hole in our hearts, perhaps especially when someone so dear to us has died tragically and unexpectedly. I am thinking of a family who lost their child due to a drunken driver, another whose five-year-old was run over accidentally by a family member, and a third whose child dove into a pond, hit his head on a rock, and is paralyzed from the neck down. It can be so easy to lose faith in the wake of these and similar tragedies.

In my life as a priest, I have seen that although the hole in the heart is like a permanent cavern and seemingly unhealable, I have witnessed truly amazing grace, deepened faith, and a desire for living. People who have experienced profound tragedy and loss are, by God's grace, often able to help others who are in the abyss of loss, who may see no future hope and may even want to die themselves. Lord, You too understand the depths of suffering and would have prayed Psalm 88, "My one companion is darkness." What we cannot understand, help us (by Your grace) to live through that which is unsurmountable, that which is so dark, and help us to never lose sight of You, our only Light and Hope.

Jesus, help me to understand and accept whatever crosses come my way, the ones I have inflicted upon myself, those caused by another, and those allowed by You. You have gone before us, carried Your cross, and showed us what it is to carry ours. May our crosses, light or burdensome, become a means to deeper conversion to You. Jesus, I trust in You!

BROKEN, YET WHOLE — 19

In Catholic theology, Hope is one of the three theological virtues. What this means, along with faith and love (charity), is that they have God as their proper object. With God's grace, these virtues elevate the human person beyond what is possible by nature alone toward the perfection that God alone possesses. As the Catechism states, hope is defined (in simplest terms) as "confident expectation." Humble sinners realize that they need this God-given gift. The self-righteous and self-deceived believe, in their own minds, that they are already saved and need little assistance.

If I've heard it once in my priesthood, I've heard it at least fifty times: "I don't need to go to confession. I've never killed anyone!" (As if murder is the only sin.) Maybe we've never committed the act of murder, but perhaps we have killed someone with our words or destroyed someone's reputation by something we've said. Perhaps we've never broken into someone's house, but we have robbed and stolen by taking advantage of people. Maybe we don't normally take the name of the Lord in vain, but we haven't spoken very highly of Him either, and we will be silent as a mouse if our faith is criticized or questioned. When we live confidently in this world in anticipation of the world to come, it changes everything: the way we speak, act, dress, think, and talk. As Dr. Scott Hahn once quipped, "It even affects the way we comb our hair!"

We hear so often, especially today, that there is no objective, revealed truth; that truth is subjective, self-defined. What is true for you may or may not be true for me. Stemming from this very prevalent manner of thinking, a wide door has been thrust open to the very popular expression so often heard today, "I'm spiritual but not religious." The word religion comes from the Latin word "*religare.*" The word from the Latin means "to unite, to bind, to connect." A person who says he or she is "spiritual but not religious" is saying (likely not consciously), "I'm spiritual but not *connected.*" They would say they possess some spiritual feelings or experiences that may or may not include prayer or a personal relationship with God. More often than not, they do not belong to any organized or revealed religious body or church.

This spirituality has, in fact, led to a great disconnect from Christ and revealed truth, and it has, instead, brought about a self-created, completely subjective "religion." Hopefully, the small seeds of this very popular spirituality will grow into a greater desire and hope to discover Truth Itself in Christ.

What determines how we speak, act, dress, think, and talk? Much can be expressed here, but thus far, nothing has been said about *conscience*. When faith in Christ is lived fully and authentically, then we are fully and authentically different. Our manner of thinking is no longer worldly, and we are configured to Christ and the things of God.

The word "conscience" comes from two Latin words, "*con*" (meaning "with") and "*scientia*" (meaning "science" or "knowledge"). The word, conscience, literally means "with science" or "with knowledge." How our conscience is formed is determined by that to which we are exposed — what we take in — the cultural air we breathe. If the only realities we are exposed to are those that the secular society and media continually present (or in reality, *force* upon us), can we then be surprised when we see all the moral disorder in the world? No wonder our children and grandchildren are so confused and disturbed. The popular adage, "You are what you eat" is true for the body, but it is also true for the soul. A properly formed conscience is achieved by being exposed to the revealed teaching of Christ and the Church. When lived in conjunction with the gift of faith, we are then positioned as persons to live fully and properly: to have hope that this world is simply a preparation for the next.

A prostitute in New York once called Archbishop Sheen and asked to meet with him. She said to him, "I am the worst girl in the city of New York." "No, you're not," he said. "You're not the worst girl in the city of New York because the worst girl in the city of New York says that she is the *best* girl in the city of New York." In other words, pride is the greatest sin. Humility and an honest realization of both our own sinfulness as well as our intrinsic dignity are a gateway to Divine hope. We are then confidently and joyfully on a beautiful journey to God.

Despair is not of God; hope *is*, because hope believes in the future. Despair is a terrible plague that brings great sadness to the soul, because it does not see a future: no future light, peace, or joy. Not only will tomorrow be the same as (or worse than) today, but the person in despair often looks far into the future and envisions no escape from their current misery and darkness. Sadly, this sometimes results in suicide or other destructive behaviors.

Many of our young people suffer from a severe level of sadness. There are a number of reasons for this. Some of this can be attributed to the economic climate of the day. They look ahead and see little possibility of finding a good paying job, being able to buy a house or support a family. They may already be in severe debt from college loans, and at their young age, already begin to see no way out. Some of their sadness may be due to political unrest or wars throughout the world. Many are truly fearful of the world in which we live and afraid that something devastating lies ahead. I have even heard it said, "I'm afraid to bring a baby into this world." They fear that their children will not have a peaceful future, or in extreme, that the world will end in their lifetime. Lastly, a profound source of despair is caused by sin and hurtful decisions that perhaps cannot be reversed. Society, and even their own misguided parents may never have taught them to live otherwise.

We pray that economic and political influences change for the better, but even if they don't, people who have found Christ will experience, in the depth of their persons, a future brightness and peace and the desire to live for tomorrow despite the pain of today. The world all around us can be collapsing, but when a person lives in Christian hope, light can still be seen and experienced – even in the midst of darkness.

Scripture says, "Hope does not disappoint, because God's love has been poured out into our hearts through the Holy Spirit, whom He has given to us" (Romans 5:5). We also know from the very words of Jesus, "With God, all things are possible" (Matthew 19:26). Whether we be the greatest of sinners or people who truly believe they have no sin, or every sinner in between, we pray for the gift of Divine hope that the world tilts toward the Lord and comes to a knowledge and love of God and of His Son, Jesus Christ, the Savior of the world.

With Divine hope, the future is not a life tilted *away* from God, but one that *faces* Him and allows us, by grace, to be drawn into His merciful light and love. We can begin to experience the beginning of heavenly joy in this world and look ahead to its fullness in the life to come. Yes indeed, with God in our lives, in our todays and our tomorrows, complete with joys and sorrows, with confident expectation, we can sing, "*It's going to be a bright, bright, bright, bright sun-shiny day!*"

THE CAUTION OF CONVERSION (WILL YOU ANSWER THE DOOR?) 20

The above title may appear to be somewhat of a contradiction. The words "caution" and "conversion" in the same sentence? After all, conversion to Christ is always good and beautiful, isn't it? Of course it is. The change in a person's life, the turning away from whatever it is that has tilted us away from God and now back to God, is always a blessing. Darkness, sin, and gloom never bring happiness or peace. Faith in Christ and the light that radiates from knowledge and love of Him always does. What is it that keeps us away? Many of these "attractions" have already been discussed: sin, addiction, excessive love of self, indifference, constant desire for comfort… the list goes on.

We have not yet discussed a very common scenario: namely, the person who is not currently living a life of faith in God but is in a secular way, still a very good person. These people abide by the Golden Rule. They treat others the way they would want to be treated. They possess what the Church defines as the "natural virtues:" virtues that can be lived on the human level without God's direct assistance. Of the natural virtues, the principal ones are called the cardinal virtues. Of course, by the very fact that all life comes from God, and indeed every breath is a Divine gift, God is the First Cause of everything. That being said, the cardinal virtues of temperance, justice, fortitude, and prudence are virtues that can be practiced and deepened simply by living with a conscientiousness of goodness and practice of virtue rather than evil.

At its most basic level, goodness brings with it an interior peace and happiness. Evil acts never do. These four basic virtues from which all other moral virtues flow (sort of like four "umbrella virtues") can and *should* be practiced by everyone: the Christian, the Jew, the Hindu, the Muslim, the Buddhist, and the unbeliever.

Justice is the virtue by which we give all people their just due. A just employer respects and takes care of his employees and does not treat them like machines, simply as a means to his own personal profit. Justice means we are treating others fairly and respectfully, including their property, freedoms, time, dignity, and so forth.

Prudence is the virtue whereby a person has the ability to think and to act properly with good decisions. Prudent people, for example, do not go out and buy a new and expensive truck when they, at the same time, are struggling to pay the mortgage and put food on the table. Prudent people make good, calculated decisions for their own benefit and that of others. Prudent people are not rash in their judgments and decisions.

Temperance is the virtue whereby a person lives a balanced life, in moderation and not in excess. We often hear of temperance relating to moderation in food and drink. Temperate people do not need to live the way of the worldly adage, "If some is good, more must be better." They are satisfied with a modest level of comfort. They are not always looking around to see what others have, how to "keep up with the Joneses," what to buy next, or what will make them appear greater in the eyes of others. Temperate people live a content life, and they are not continually seeking the "what's next?" of life. This is not to say that temperate people cannot, at the same time, be strivers and achievers, but they do so in a way that is not always seeking self-glorification.

Fortitude is that virtue by which a person has the interior ability, strength and courage to endure the conflicts and burdens of life, including those excesses or temptations that drag us down as human persons. People of fortitude have the ability to say "yes" when yes is necessary, and "no" when no is needed. They are able to get up each morning in the midst of life's daily struggles and not collapse under the weight that life sometimes brings. Simply stated, those who do not possess or practice the virtue of fortitude will find themselves weaker in the face of life's struggles, whereas a person of fortitude may also be carrying these same burdens but is able to stay the course.

There are many good people in the world who possess all or some of these virtues at one level or another. Some non-believers even possess them in greater abundance than Christian believers. The moral virtues are increased by frequently exercising them and diminished by lack of use. Just as a body becomes stronger through greater exercise and proper diet, so, too, the human person grows in virtue through daily practice and weaker through moral indolence.

People who practice these virtues have good qualities, and we may even call them "good" people. The world is filled with these good people, many striving to become even better and more virtuous. These people make wonderful parents, workers, citizens, and contribute greatly to society in so many ways. In terms of the spiritual life, these virtues can be practiced without the practitioner necessarily having a relationship with God. God loves us so much that He gifts even the unbeliever or the semi-believer with the ability to grow in goodness and virtue. In other words, God can infuse natural virtues by His grace.

There is, in this life, as has been discussed thus far, the supernatural gift of faith that God desires to bestow on us in abundance, because He "desires all to be saved and come to the knowledge of the truth" (1 Timothy 2:4). Many find and embrace faith; many never do. Virtues lived with a robust spiritual life (or a deep relationship with God) can go beyond what is naturally possible. In other words, God's grace gives us the ability to move beyond our own natural abilities. It is ultimately God's Divine Life that initiates this desire within us. God is patient.

In the very popular painting by the mid-nineteenth century English artist William Holman Hunt, Christ is depicted holding a lantern and knocking at a door, symbolizing the door of our hearts; however, the knob is only on the inside. Christ waits patiently for us, and conversion begins once we allow the Lord to enter. For some, the day of conversion (of tilting one's life to Christ) is as memorable as their wedding day or some other immensely significant event in their lives. For others, the door allowing Christ to enter opens slowly, and the process of change is gradual rather than sudden — more so in "baby steps" than immediate.

J. & R. Lamb Studios, Designer. *Design drawing for stained glass for Beatific memorial window showing Christ knocking at door, with lilies; William Holman Hunt illustration-style.*
(Photograph retrieved from the Library of Congress)

Now that a certain stage is set, what does the chapter "The Caution of Conversion" mean? Is there a danger or concern in this?

There can be. What happens very frequently when people are gifted with faith, especially if they were once living a tilted life far away from God, is that the pendulum of life moves from a life of little or no God to a life of nothing *but* God. This can be beautiful, of course, with the caution being that these newly formed Christians sometimes expect everyone else in their family and circle of friends and coworkers to suddenly and immediately be as they are — and believe — the same as they do.

This exuberance and enthusiasm can quickly and easily be perceived as judgmental and self-righteous, the attitude that everyone else should suddenly experience the same faith-filled life as they do. Their attitude may come across as, "I am now enlightened, and you are still a sinner." The pendulum of faith seems to have swung hard and fast from one direction to the other. For most, this is not an attractive faith attitude. It does not inspire or encourage change in others. In fact, it actually becomes a turnoff to others' faith. Many an unpleasant discussion has been created around the Thanksgiving or Christmas table when well-meaning relatives immediately impose their "holier than thou" presence and expectation upon entire families.

The people for whom this new gift has been granted need to be aware that their newfound faith is not automatic for everyone else. They need to realize that Christ was very patient with them, knocking on their door, perhaps for many years, waiting to be let in. Faith cannot be forced onto others. Per the old expression, "You can lead a horse to water, but you can't make it drink." We lead people to Christ by humbly practicing the virtues and leading an authentic, joyful life. Patience is not one of the cardinal virtues, yet patiently waiting will bear fruit; aggressive evangelization rarely will.

One of the spiritual works of mercy is to "admonish the sinner," correcting someone who is on the wrong path. There are ways to do this and ways not to — helpful ways and destructive ways. Anyone who loves other people desires what is best for them, desires their good. The last thing we want to witness is those whom we love making destructive decisions — decisions that can sometimes negatively affect the rest of their lives.

We can sometimes see very clearly what another cannot. This is especially true if our own lives and consciences are in proper order and most especially if we are already directed and ordered toward God. Correcting someone (in spiritual language known as "fraternal correction" or "fraternal charity") at the wrong time or in the wrong way can actually add insult to injury: salt on an already present wound. Improperly spoken or untimely words pound a wedge into a relationship that causes either permanent division or at least the need for deep healing. Knowing what to say and when to say it requires great wisdom and prudence, both a gift and a virtue.

There are essentially five criteria for fraternal charity. These criteria, if practiced and spoken charitably, give the best chance for people to see particular errors in their lives and hopefully make the needed and beneficial changes (conversion). The five that are given here presume an already established relationship between two people. It can happen, and does, that a complete stranger or a mere acquaintance corrects something he or she sees in our lives. If we hear it in humility, instead of saying, "Who are YOU to tell ME what to do?," we may have the grace to recollect our actions and make the necessary change for the better. This form of correction is rare.

The following five criteria are built on relationships and are the most common. First and foremost, before correcting someone, we must ask ourselves:

1. Is the matter under question of a serious nature? Is it detrimental? If it is not, you may want to simply "let it go." Previously mentioned, as Pope St. John XXIII once said, "See everything, criticize little, overlook much." In modern language, don't "sweat the small stuff" or make a mountain out of a molehill. Sometimes it simply is not worth it. At other times, it is, indeed, worth it, and little corrections like, "Did you know that you chew with your mouth open?" can save a person from a great deal of future embarrassment. Hopefully, our words will be received gratefully and will be truly beneficial to a person's future. Other corrections are of a more serious nature. "Why is it that you no longer go to church?" or "You have a serious drinking problem that is destroying yourself and your family." Before being directly addressed, these corrections need to be prepared for with great prayer.

2. Am I the best person to make the correction? I may be, but perhaps someone else would be more effective: a grandparent, co-worker, or friend. The best chance for the desired response is when the correction is made in charity from a person who truly loves the wrongdoer. What a wife says to a husband may fall on deaf ears, but if his golfing buddy says the same thing, it may bear different fruit.

3. Is now the right time? Is it the proper place and setting? These are important questions. We have all heard the expression, "timing is everything." It is very true when it comes to correction. If the time and place are not appropriate, then wait for the time that is. After a hard day's work may not be the best time to tell someone that he or she never helps out around the house. If a person is grieving the loss of another, it is probably not the ideal time to say, "You have been spending too much money on lottery tickets."

4. Do I have the proper motivation? If my motivation is not so much fraternal charity, but rather, "one-upping," or proving "I'm right, you're wrong," then keep silent. Otherwise, you risk doing more harm than good. This attitude is actually a poor reflection on you and an area of your life that needs to be looked at. Keep in mind, when we point one of our five fingers at another person, four of them are pointing back at us. True love desires the good of another.

5. Does my correction have a reasonable possibility for the desired outcome? If not, then now is not the time. Sometimes, people are so far removed from hearing the truth about themselves, that our words simply don't register. Spiritual blindness distorts our vision of self, and in fact, distorts our vision of all of reality. As with St. Paul, the scales covering our eyes need to be peeled away so we can see clearly the path of life with God. God can break through the most distant heart.

A common example today is when parents are distraught (or at least very disturbed) knowing that their child is living with someone outside of marriage, or that their upcoming marriage will be nonsacramental and performed in a location other than a church. Your children already know how you feel, and if you raised them in a faith-filled home, they may even know that it hurts you. Our culture truly sees nothing wrong with this, and this is a moral blindness. After expressing your heartfelt opinion as a parent, continually hammering them with words of disappointment or even anger rarely, if ever, succeeds. There comes a point when you begin to realize that the best you can do is pray for them and lead by joyful example. How often it happens that even many years later, people who have, by grace, discovered a new way of looking at life, come to see a priest to talk about decisions made in younger years. Always have hope that this change of heart can happen in the lives of your loved ones too.

Dr. Bernard Nathanson, the very well-known New York abortion doctor who was responsible for tens of thousands of abortions, one day saw the light and his life immediately changed. He died a faith-filled, practicing Catholic. In the decades previous to this, he was blind, and speaking to him about abortion would have likely yielded little or no fruit. The Holy Spirit entered his heart, and the prayers of many were answered.

If we are to attempt to be an instrument of change in a person's life through our words, all of the above questions should ideally first be asked in prayer. Very often, when we act on our own, without God being anywhere in the mix, we act rashly and imprudently. Prayer is not only the fertilizer for our souls, it is the soil, the water, and the sunlight. True spiritual change and growth will not happen without it.

There have been several times in my life both as a priest and as a lay person, when I have, in charity, corrected another. Most of these instances were humbly received, but one or two were not, at least at the time of correction. The five methods described above are not failsafe but a good guideline to follow. Much depends upon the humble disposition of the one receiving the correction.

There is one "correction" story that occurred in my life that is worth sharing. This was not a situation of a moral fault in the life of another, but it was still a correction that certainly helped the man. I was twenty-five years old and was meeting with a priest who was nearly sixty. He was the rector of the Dominican House of Studies in Washington, D.C., and I was a student. He was a wonderful priest and mentor to so many. He was also an excellent preacher, and part of his ministry was to give parish missions in many places throughout the country.

However, he had a very unusual habit. When he preached, his tongue would often come out of his mouth and make a full circle all around his lips. It was extremely distracting, at least to me, but everyone in any congregation certainly saw it. At the end of our meeting, he asked me if I had any questions. (I was twenty-five; he was sixty.) Who was I to correct someone whom I perceived as a spiritual giant? But the words just came out. Perhaps it was the Holy Spirit, but I said to him, "Not a question, but a comment. I love your preaching [I was at least smart enough to start with a compliment!], but did you realize when you preach that your tongue comes out of your mouth?" "WHAT!?" he exclaimed. With a bit of shock, he said, "What do you mean? Show me." So in his presence, I put my tongue out and did a "lap" around my lips. "WHAT?" he cried anew, and then asked, "How many times?" Now wanting to get out of the hot seat in which I had just placed myself and wishing it were all over, I slowly responded, "In the course of a homily, maybe fifteen times." "WHAT!?" he exclaimed a third time, now much more loudly. After a brief pause, he said, "I have been ordained a priest for nearly forty years and no one has ever told me that."

He then proceeded to thank me. I was later told that the following year, when he was preaching a homily on fraternal charity to the entire student body at the seminary, he used this story as an example. Fraternal charity is almost always awkward and difficult, but if the proper conditions are met and with the grace of the Holy Spirit, it can bear great change, conversion, and new direction in a person's life. If accepted with a spirit of humility, the recipients will be forever grateful.

MEND YOUR NETS   21

As I come to the close of this little book on conversion to Christ, I am sitting in a beautiful chapel in Magdala overlooking the Sea of Galilee. It was from this small fishing town that Mary Magdalene, a woman immersed in sin, first encountered Jesus. When she did, everything in her life changed. The once distorted attractiveness of sin that possessed her with seven demons was now behind her. Through this encounter with Christ, her desires and motivations, once thought to bring happiness, were immediately discovered to be a distortion of reality and a lie.

Altar of Boat Chapel, Duc in Altum, Magdala, Israel (2022)

Through these pages, we have discovered that until we discover Christ, we will, in one way or another, follow what the world offers. Much of what the world offers is very good. The opening pages of the Bible, the Book of Genesis, speak of God's creation as being "good" and of mankind as "very good." In fact, it is here in this created world where we discover Christ, the meaning and purpose of life. If, as Shakespeare says, *"All the world is a stage,"* (As You Like It, Act II, scene vii) then the world *itself* is a theatre — a theatre of God's redemption. For it is here in this life where we have the opportunity to develop an intimate relationship with God.

This world, however, is merely a preparation for the best that is yet to come — an appetizer, so to speak — when in fact, a heavenly banquet awaits us. The world also offers many allurements. Mary Magdalene and so many others with her throughout the ages and even to the present day have followed the enticements of the world. They have either suffered the effects of sinful choices or have settled for an existence of mediocrity and limited happiness. Mary Magdalene, thankfully by God's grace, experienced a *metanoia*, a complete change of heart. May all reading this brief book find themselves in the position of Mary: to find Christ who awakens the dead soul, brings light to the darkened mind, and abundant life to the blind of spirit.

Perfect contrition is sorrow for sin arising from perfect love. It arises from a love by which God is loved above all else. Imperfect contrition is sorrow for sin, not so much because we have offended Love Itself, but rather sorrow out of fear of punishment. Both suffice as an expression of sorrow, with the first being the goal of the Christian and greater than the latter. In the same way, living one's life devoted to God and neighbor greatly benefits the soul and objectively is "better" than "cramming for the finals," as my late dad once said. God, in His infinite mercy, can make saints from those "hired in the last hour." "These have only worked one hour, and you have made them equal to us who have borne the burden of the work in the scorching heat of the day" (Matthew 20:12). There are indeed many paths to Christ. Mary Magdalene's change in life was ultimately the result of falling in love with Christ.

Our Catholic faith humbly teaches that we, as a Church, truly possess the fullness of Revelation. The Church provides through its teaching and Sacramental life, the means to encounter Christ and ultimately, *the* means to salvation. At the Good Friday liturgy, the Church throughout the world prays for separated Christians along with those who do not profess any faith in Christ or have no belief in God whatsoever. The Church recognizes all good and is constantly spreading seeds: a "Divine farmer" praying that some seeds take root.

With all this said, the faith journey to God is never a cookie-cutter approach. The majority of people do not begin a life of faith as children and continue to grow throughout their lives. We are often distracted or even broken. One size does not fit all, and your path will indeed be unique as you are unique: precious and unrepeatable. Christ continually calls —that is true— yet, very often the necessary grace for deeper intimacy with God comes at that time when we are most open to receive it: when it will finally take root. Perhaps for you it is now, at this time in your life.

Priests ought to pray for the many souls who have crossed the threshold of a church, perhaps, for the first time, because they are now in the house of God (a home court advantage, so to speak), and the Lord can touch the distant, hurting, or rebellious heart. The spark of Divine Life can enter the soul, and like Mary Magdalene, the God who was never sought may now become the sole desire of one's heart. Christ suffered and died for all. The practicing Christian needs continual conversion, because we are all weak; how much weaker, then, are those who neither seek nor even want God? Christ, who can do all things, desires to break the will of even the most hardened heart, "taking away our stony hearts and giving us natural hearts" (Ezekiel 36:26).

Those of us in good health, both bodily and spiritually, rarely have a clue as to what it must be like to live in pain, physical or emotional, day after day. We sympathize with and pray for those who are suffering and are unable to see or understand its deeper meaning, its potential for bringing us to a deeper love of God and sharing in His redemptive suffering. This can be intensely difficult for the *faithful* Christian; how much more difficult it must be for the person who does not yet understand the Cross!

It is the mature soul, the soul that loves Christ deeply, that is able to do so—sometimes even with joy. This is a much deeper spirituality, one of the highest states of the spiritual life. When our suffering is offered to God and configured to His suffering, it begins the making of a great saint. If I ever have the joy of writing another book, perhaps it will be about this most difficult, yet least understood mystery of Christian living.

Along with the new heart of Mary Magdalene, it was also from this little fishing town as well as nearby Capernaum, that the apostles were taught to be fishers of men. We will all, one day, be faced with the questions, "Where did you cast your net? What was it in life that you were fishing for and hoping to catch?" Have you perhaps been dropping your net in the wrong places and coming up empty? Searching and never quite finding? In the words of Luke 5:4, and beautifully repeated by Pope St. John Paul II, *Duc In Altum* — "put out into the deep." These words encourage us to move from the shallow and murky waters where humanity all too often finds itself and to "tilt" and discover the rich depth of faith in Christ. After a night of fishing, Christ told his disciples, "Cast your nets on the right side of the boat" (John 21:6). May we not only discover the abundant catch that Christ promises, but by His grace, also teach others to do the same — one degree at a time.